One Foot in the Sea

D0233453

To Meg and Sandy,
with love and
best wishes.

Other books by Robert Smith
Grampian Ways
Discovering Aberdeenshire
Valley of the Dee
The Granite City
The Royal Glens

One Foot in the Sea

ROBERT SMITH

JOHN DONALD PUBLISHERS LTD
EDINBURGH

ISBN 0 85976 342 0

British Library Cataloguing in Publication Data
A catalogue record for this book is available from the British Library.

Typeset by the Midlands Book Typesetting Company, Loughborough
Printed in Great Britain by Arrowsmith Ltd., Bristol

Acknowledgements

This book draws on the experience, memories, knowledge and writings of many people. I am grateful to all those who showed me the way along the North-east coastal trail.
Aberdeen, 1991   Robert Smith

One foot in sea, and one on shore,
To one thing constant never.
William Shakespeare,
Much Ado about Nothing.

Contents

CHAPTER ONE

Coarse Fisher Brutes

From the cliffs at St Cyrus you can look out across the wide sweep of Montrose Bay to where the North Esk tumbles into the sea south of a ragged saltmarsh known as the Slunks. Down there among the white-washed salmon fishers' bothies at Kirkside is the old kirkyard of Ecclesgreig, the 'church of the rock', crouched under a semi-circle of basalt cliffs called the Steeples. Before the roadside community of St Cyrus developed on top of the cliffs, this was the heart of the parish.

Ecclesgreig was the starting point of a journey that was to take me round the 'knuckle' of Scotland, the great finger of land thrusting out into the sea at Kinnaird Head in Buchan. From Kirkside I would go north through the red clay lands of the Mearns, on to Fraserburgh and Peterhead, and west by the old fisher towns of Banffshire to Findhorn Bay and the sands of Culbin. I was to learn about flooks and poddlers, mermaids and monsters, 'selkies' and sea dogs, and a good deal more, but down in the old kirkyard, where it all began, 'ghaists and spectres, wan and pale' were waiting for me.

Under the Steeples, ferns claw their way over the kirkyard wall as if trying to blot out the memory of what happened there more than a century and a half ago. If the old tales are true, will-o'-the-wisps and wirriekows were to be seen rollicking around the Ecclesgreig tombstones after dark. George Beattie, a lawyer-poet from Montrose, wrote about them in a poem called 'John o' Arnha', which owed a good deal to Burns's 'Tam o' Shanter'. Then he created a gory legend of his own – one that the Bard never equalled. He walked to the Auld Kirkyard, sat down by its crooked stile, and blew his brains out.

Despite his fascination with ghosts that 'clappit their wither'd hands', kelpies with 'twa bullock's horns', dragons' tails and joints of steel, and old hags who rode out of the Slunks on 'broomstick nags', Beattie was no merchant of gloom. He had a reputation as a wit, walked about with a pet jackdaw on his shoulder, and liked to play practical jokes. On one occasion he was blamed for removing all the street lamps of Montrose from their lamp posts during the night.

'John o' Arnha' was based on a splay-footed town officer called John Finlay. John, with his red coat, knee breeches and broad-brimmed hat, was a familiar figure in Montrose. He was married five times, and when he was asked which wife he liked best he replied that he 'aye liket the livin' ane'. George Beattie was less lucky in love, and he 'liket' only one woman. He had arranged to marry the daughter of a local farmer, but her ardour cooled when she inherited a large sum of money. She jilted him for a prosperous corn merchant.

Beattie wrote a long, sad poem in which he told her she would soon be rid of him. On the night of 29 September, 1823, he made his way down the cliff path and walked along the links to Ecclesgreig. That night a storm broke over St Cyrus, howling across the sand dunes and beating itself out against the cliffs behind the kirkyard. It was a night for 'ghaists and spectres'. I have often wondered if the doomed lawyer-poet saw his own ghoulish creations 'dance in dead array' before him as he sat staring across the dark hollow of the Slunks. Next morning, a herd boy called Willie Balfour found him propped against the dyke with his hands on his chest, a pistol at his mouth, and the thumb of his right hand on the trigger.

Beattie's grave is almost on the spot where he shot himself. The inscription on his tombstone says he was charitable, benevolent, fair, independent, forcible and pathetic. His manners were 'plain and social'. Few people come to see the grave. Fewer still know of the poem written by the man who lies there. The ghosts have been banished from Kirkside.

Thousands of people visit St Cyrus each year, some for birds, some for botany. It is now a nature reserve, a breeding ground for the little tern, the rarest tern in Britain, and an important botanical site. The St Cyrus beach must be one of the loveliest in Britain, and certainly the most unspoiled. Near the salmon bothy, a wooden bridge built by a troop of Ghurkas takes visitors across the Slunks to the sands. The Slunks (the word means a wet and muddy hollow) was the bed of the North Esk before it changed course, for at one time it flowed northwards past the churchyard on its way to the sea.

The places mentioned in Beattie's poem are still there ... the Auld Kirk of Logie, Martin's Den, the Ponnage pool, the Stone of Morphie. There is a farm called the Stone of Morphie, which took its name from a huge monolith standing in the farm courtyard, a reminder of the kelpie's complaint that he had a 'sair back and sair banes' from carrying the Laird o' Morphie's stones.

In Martin's Den there is a beech tree with the name of another poet who knew all about the Ponnage Pool, and who saw it with less fearful eyes, when it was 'bricht wi' the floor o' the yallow mim'lus'. Helen Cruickshank, who was once described as Scotland's best loved modern poet, was walking in the Den with her younger brother Will when he carved her name on the tree – it was their last walk together.

I mind o' the Ponnage Pool
The reid brae risin',
Morphy Lade,
An' the salmon that louped the dam,
A tree i' Martin's Den
Wi' names carved on it;
But I ken na wha I am.
Ane o' the names was mine,
An' still I own it.

In that poem, 'The Ponnage Pool', she wrote about the martin fleein' across the River Esk, but Martin's Den takes its name from a different kind of martin – a saint, not a bird. The Kirk of Logie was dedicated to St Martin, and there is a well in the den known as St Martin's Well, which is said to have medicinal properties. Bob Cooper, who lives and works on Mains of Logie farm, pointed across the fields to the Den and recalled how he had scrambled down its steep slopes to cool himself at the well in the hot summer days of his youth. An extension to his cottage has blotted out the old name of the building, cut out on one of the stones – Martin's Villa.

The road to the Kirk of Logie, where the witches Elspet and Mauzie cantered about on their 'broomstick nags', runs downhill behind Bob's cottage. The Kirk, roofless now, lies below the farmhouse. It is a small, quaint building, quiet and peaceful, but on a dark and stormy night it would be easy to imagine ghouls and ghosties chasing each other around its lurching tombstones. A track runs past its gates to the banks of the Esk, where, if you listen carefully, you may hear the Kelpie howling in the Ponnage Pool.

Helen Cruickshank became a much respected figure in the Scottish literary scene. Among her friends were Hugh Macdiarmid, Edwin Muir and Lewis Grassic Gibbon. She knew both Marion Angus and the Angus poet Violet Jacob, who wrote so hauntingly about 'the saft mist o' the morn' on Craigo Woods. The woods were no great distance from Helen's birthplace at Hillside. Because she thought they were sacred to Violet Jacob, she never used the name in her own verse, although it was her 'nearest and dearest woodland Sunday walk'. She died in 1975 at the age of 88.

Helen's parents worked at Sunnyside Royal Hospital at Hillside. When 'The Ponnage Pool' was published in 1968, coinciding with her 82nd birthday, she went back to Montrose after an absence of nearly half a century. She was taken down to the river by the hospital's medical superintendent to look again at the pool she had written about.

'The herbage seemed coarser than I remembered', she wrote in her *Octobiography*, 'but there was still "a martin fleein across" to the nests under the reid brae of Morphie on the far side of the North Esk'. Bob Cooper told me that not many people in the Logie area knew about the Ponnage Pool, or even its whereabouts, for they were mostly incomers, and it turned out that he was right. Elspet and Mauzie seem to have mounted their broomstick nags and ridden off into the misty Land of Make-Believe.

Helen Cruickshank wrote about the salmon running up the Esk from the sea, but over on the shore they were loupin' less briskly when I was there. Out on the sands a spider web of salmon nets lay along the sea edge, tiny figures picking their way precariously across the ropes. 'What are they doing?' asked a visitor. They were cleaning the nets. Jim Ritchie, who has been fishing there since 1947, told me there had been a drop in the season's catch. 'Northumberland's been grabbing them,' he said. Not so long ago they were taking out 4,000 grilse and 2,000 salmon in a season. 'We used to take out 7,000,' said Jim. I was to hear the same story all round the north-east coast. Salmon fishing has always been part of the St Cyrus scene. Three centuries ago the barons in their castles at Morphie and Lauriston boiled and pickled and packed them in barrels for markets in the Baltic and the Netherlands and fed their servants with what was left. But the main centre of activity was less than two miles north of St Cyrus, at Miltonhaven.

Miltonhaven, which had weekly markets and fairs twice a year, one of them a four-day event drawing crowds from all over the Mearns, boasted more than 50 houses and 170 inhabitants. Some were white fishers, competing with Johnshaven farther up the coast, but the Mathers community owed its prosperity largely to lime and smuggling.

At the end of the 17th century, when lime was becoming increasingly important as a fertiliser, the biggest limekiln Scotland had ever seen was built at Boddin Point, on the northern point of Lunan Bay, by Robert Scott of Dunninald. This great castle-like structure was erected in 1696 and extended in 1750. It was in the latter year that Scott, looking for new commercial prospects, turned his attention to Miltonhaven, where a long reef of limestone rock stretched across the bay. He built a kiln on the shore and began blasting the reef. It paid rich dividends, for Miltonhaven flourished and its population doubled.

But if lime put new life into Miltonhaven, it also killed it. The limestone reef, which acted as a barrier to the incoming waves, became perilously thin, and in the early 1790s the sea broke through it, carrying away part of the village. A wall was built to keep the sea out, but by 1792 the remaining cottages, the lime workings and the harbour had disappeared. Today, there is nothing to show that it ever existed.

Tiny 'Tanglelia' lies just south of Miltonhaven. It was built to replace the 'drowned' village, but it never got beyond what it is today, a cluster of neat cottages on the sea's watery doorstep. It is cluttered with lobster pots, nets and fishing gear, and the tangle that gave it its name spreads in dark, dank lines across its stony shore. It was from Tangleha' that I made my way round to the Rock Hall fishing station, where I was looking for the Kaim of Mathers, or what was left of it. This old castle sticks up like a gnarled thumb on a cliff-top site near the St Cyrus sands, guarded by crumbling battlements. Rock Hall itself is a peaceful place, a buffer between St Cyrus beach and Miltonhaven, but it has a grisly past.

George Beattie, with all his ghosts and goblins, could never have dreamed up the horror that hangs over the shattered fortalice in this little bay. It was built by David Barclay of Mathers during the reign of James I of Scotland, after the laird had angered the king by brutally murdering James Melville of Glenbervie, Sheriff of the Mearns. Melville was detested by the local lairds, who repeatedly complained to the king about his high-handed behaviour. Without thinking, the king remarked, 'Sorrow gin he were sodden and supped in bree'. In other words, for all he cared they could go and make soup of him.

So that was what the Mearns lairds did. Four of them – the lairds of Mathers, Lauriston, Arbuthnott and Pittarrow – invited the sheriff to a hunting party in the forest of Garvock, kindled a fire, and boiled a huge cauldron of water over it, then they seized the sheriff, stripped him naked, and threw him into the boiling water. Afterwards, each man supped from the ghastly brew. In *Cloud Howe*, Lewis Grassic Gibbon described in gruesome detail how the doomed sheriff, howling like a wolf in the water, slowly ceased to 'scraich', his body 'bloated red as the clay, till the flesh loosed off from his seething bones'.

The King, angry that his remark had been taken so literally, denounced them as outlaws, vowing that Barclay would never be given peace to live either on land or sea. The laird of Mathers shut himself up in his cliff-top eyrie at St Cyrus, but he was eventually pardoned. The thought of that bloated red body floating in the great pot on Garvock Hill must have lingered in his mind, for he swore that if ever again he supped broth he would expect the same sort of treatment that had been meted out to Sheriff Melville.

The spot where the four lairds drank their cannibal brew is about two miles south-east of Fordoun at Brownies' Hollow, which was said to be haunted by brownies after the murder. The farm of Brownies Leys is nearby, not on the Hill of Garvock, but lying in the shadow of Kenshot Hill. No one lives there now. The deserted farm buildings are in ruins, the wind moaning through shattered windows and broken doors as if sounding a dirge for the terrible thing that happened there all those years ago. Outside the empty farmhouse, seeing something move among the trees, I wondered if brownies were still hanging around the scene of the crime, but the 'ghost' was more substantial than that. Sandy Reid was feeding his cattle.

Sandy, who owns the farm of Sillyflat outside Bervie, bought Brownie Leys about ten years ago. He pointed out what was supposed to be the actual site, an overgrown hollow or gully with a burn running through it at the bottom of his farm road. At one time it was known as the Sheriff's Kettle. He had often wondered what he would find if he took a digger and tried to lift the 'lid' of the kettle.

The word *kaim* means a fortress, or a ridge of hills, and the Hill of Garvock is a long, unspectacular ridge on the north-eastern flank of the Howe of Mearns, with striking panoramic views of the surrounding countryside. One theory is that the name refers to pinnacles resembling a cock's comb, or *kaim*. At any rate, Gibbon used it in both senses. He was always drawn to the hills.

Five miles north of Garvock is a hill called Bruxie. Bruxie was mentioned by Gibbon in *Sunset Song*, but not by name, only as 'a great flat hill-top'. There was 'a bit loch' there, a 'woesome dark stretch fringed rank with rushes and knifegrass'. I wanted to see this 'spleiter of water', so I set off for Bruxie Hill over the narrow, twisting roads that run west from Catterline. At one time you could get to it from a farm track going up by Pitforthie, but today the easiest approach is from the north side of Bruxie Hill, branching off the main A94 road to Laurencekirk.

The road to Bruxie goes past Meetlaw, which a Buchan man, Jim Cumming, from New Deer, has farmed for over 20 years. He told me he was now 'kind o' retired'. I had Cummine relatives in Buchan and we exchanged notes about our Comyn forbears. The Ordnance Survey map has two lochs on Bruxie, although Gibbon mentioned only one. There *were* two, but both have dried up, although the rushes still trace the outlines of the lochs. It was said that one of them was bottomless. In *Sunset Song*, Long Robb of the Mill remarked that if the loch had no bottom to it that made it like the depths of a parson's depravity.

Jim Cumming found a bottom to both lochs. He drained them about ten years ago, partly because he wanted the land and partly because his cattle were always falling into them. Not that he had any qualms about doing it, or that anyone mourned their going, for according to Jim no one climbs up Bruxie Hill nowadays looking for the ghosts of Blawearie and Peesie's Knapp. Yet it was up on that windy hill, looking out over the farms and crofts that stretch away to the coast, that Gibbon found his inspiration. 'Coarse land and lonely', he called it, and up there on Bruxie, where the snipe drummed out their evening call, deafening him with their noise, he gazed across the hill to a circle of stones that stood near the loch, thinking about the 'coarse devils' of Druids who sang foul heathen songs around them so many years ago.

Over on the south side of Bruxie Hill, at Nether Pitforthie, a road goes plunging down over the Reisk to Arbuthnott, passing a farm track with the sign Hareden at the end of it, while a little farther on is Bloomfield, where Leslie Mitchell spent his childhood. Bloomfield was the Blawearie of *Sunset Song* and Robert Middleton, the Mitchell's neighbour at Hareden, was immortalised as Long Rob of the Mill. There is no sign of a mill at Hareden, and its whereabouts is a bit of a mystery. Jim Cumming thought that the loch on Bruxie Hill had been used as a dam for a meal mill, although he wasn't sure where it had been. There is, in fact, the remains of a stone wall on Bruxie, which suggests that he may have been correct.

There is little left on that remote stretch of road on the Reisk to evoke any real sense of the Mearns that Gibbon knew as a child. The horse and plough no longer cut great furrows across the land, and any romantic notion you might have of Blawearie dies with the clatter of tractors crawling like ugly beetles over the Bervie braes. The croft house at Hareden has become a bungalow and Bloomfield itself has few echoes of the 'fell brave house' with three beech trees and hedges 'bonny with honeysuckle'. At one time, there was talk of turning it into a museum, but the idea was dropped in favour of a visitors' centre at Arbuthnott.

Yet there is still something about the real-life Blawearie that leaves its mark on you, partly because this was the heart of *Sunset Song* and *Cloud Howe*, but mostly because it is the place where James Leslie Mitchell was brought up, where he spent his childhood, helped to wrest a living from the 'weary pleiter of the land', and pedalled away over dusty roads searching for his dreams on a bike he called his 'clank-and-growl'. It was here that he crossed the fields to Hareden to see his childhood sweetheart, and where he listened to Robert Middleton talking about horses – he could tell you stories about horses, they said, 'till you'd fair be grey in the head'. In Gibbon's school essays, this corner of the Mearns is seen through the boy's eyes ... the 'long white winding road' that ran through fields and moors belonging to the farms of Kirkton and Pitcarles, the town of Bervie with its 'smoking factories and a few fishing boats dotting the sea beyond', and the distant hills covered with yellow broom.

The rough stone road that went wandering 'out of the world and into Blawearie' was well-known to young Leslie Mitchell, as well as to Rebecca Middleton at Hareden, who was to grow up and marry him. They tramped up and down it every day on their way to Arbuthnott School, and it was at Arbuthnott that Mitchell found a headmaster, Alexander Gray, who was to play an important part in moulding both his character and his talent.

Coming down over the Reisk, I passed a farm called Gobbs. The name might have been plucked from the pages of *Sunset*

Song, along with Cuddiestoun and Meiklebogs and all the other dour-sounding names in Gibbon's novels. A bit farther on, I turned a corner and saw the rooftops of Inverbervie. It struck me then that Gibbon had been very near to the sea at Bloomfield, only four or five miles at the most. It was the land that possesed him; he liked, he said, 'this idle task of voyaging with a pen through the storm-happed wastes of Scotland'. But in the last years of his life his voyaging took him away from the land, closer to the coast, where he could hear the 'yammer of seagulls' and watch the tide 'frothing and swishing green into the caves'. Gibbon's last, unfinished novel, *The Speak of the Mearns*, was set along the inhospitable coastline that runs its ragged course from the mouth of the North Esk to Dunnottar Castle.

Gibbon, thirled to the land, paid only passing attention to the fishing communities in his earlier works, but two towns on the Mearns coast felt the full blast of the rancour that made him 'the speak of the place'. One was Stonehaven, 'Steenie', the home of the 'poverty toffs', where you might live in sin as much as you pleased but were damned to hell if you hadn't a white sark. He thought that the Mearns capital was 'awful proud of its sarks but not of its slums'.

The other town was Gourdon, three miles north of Johnshaven, Gourdon has always run against the tide. It was the first village in Scotland to adopt the motor boat in preference to the steam drifter. Ten years ago over a score of dual-purpose motor fishing vessels landed their catches at Gourdon. Then, it was the only village still using the old hand-line method of fishing and the men freely admitted that they owed their prosperity to their womenfolk, who each day baited 1,200 hooks with mussels. These are the women whose forbears were the butt of Gibbon's abrasive wit. 'Before a Gourdon quean speaks the truth', he said, 'the Bervie burn will run backwards through the Howe.' As for the men, these 'coarse fisher brutes', he thought they would 'wring silver out of a corpse's wame and call stinking haddocks perfume fishes'.

There is only one hand-line fishing boat in Gourdon today. The reason for the decline is that younger fishermen have married women from outside the village, '*queans*' who have no desire to spend the rest of their lives baiting hooks in back-garden sheds. The sole survivor of the hand-line fleet is the *Enterprise*, owned by Alex Welsh, who is in his early sixties. He operates it as a 'share' boat with Bob Mellis, who is sixty-three. Alex's wife, Rina, baits the hooks, 1,000 of them every day, and Bob's wife baits another 1,000. The women also have to shell the mussels, so that the whole business takes them anything from six to eight hours a day. They have to get up at five o'clock in the morning to do the job. When I was at Alex's house in Seaview Terrace there were two 'hurlies' in his back-garden, one piled high with lines waiting to be baited, the other – inside his garden shed – stacked with hooks baited and ready for the *Enterprise* the following morning. Prams used by hand-line fishermen in the past can still be seen lying about the quayside.

Gourdon is a tight little community. Alex's mother lives just off the main street, her backyard cluttered with lobster pots and barrels of empty mussel shells waiting to be dumped. Over on the quay, his brother Douglas runs the Gourline fish house, whose succulent fish, fresh from the sea, give the lie to Gibbon's 'stinking haddocks' jibe. Alex himself is a quiet and friendly man, content with his lot, brushing aside any suggestion that his is a hard life. Neither he nor anyone else I met in Gourdon looked like the 'fisher brutes' of Gibbon's taunt.

What brought such bile to the Mearns author's pen is anybody's guess, but it left scars. He was at it again in *The Speak of the Mearns*, hitting out at Stonehaven's dreichness, at its midden piles – 'the highest and feuchest' – and at the Kinneff minister's wife, 'a fusionless old gype mooning and dreaming and thinking of God and rubbish like that.' It is tantalising to consider how many people he would have offended if he had lived to complete the book. *The Speak of the Mearns*, wrote Ian Campbell, in an introduction, 'would not have made Gibbon much more popular in his native countryside than did *Sunset Song*'.

Some would have laughed it off, which would have won plus points from Gibbon. He had a soft spot for the folk of

Laurencekirk, who laughed at his jibes, not crying 'as they did in Drumlithie when you mocked at their steeple' (Gibbon said they took the steeple in when it rained), or 'smile sick and genteel as they did in Stonehaven when you spoke of the poverty toffs'. But some found it hard to laugh. They knew where Skite was, and Blawearie and Pooty's place, and to them the people in *Sunset Song* were real people. Gibbon held up a mirror to their lives, and they resented what they saw.

Even today, the resentment lingers on. The Gibbons centre at Arbuthnott was envisaged as a place where students and school pupils could come to study the writer's work. Nevertheless, some people were opposed to the idea from the start, the young as well as the old. 'I wouldn't give a penny to *that!*' they said. 'He just blackened folk here.' So, more than half a century after his death, Gibbon's work is still the speak of the place.

Arbuthnott, where a rough, tree-shaded track runs down to the Kirkton and Arbuthnott Church, is where James Leslie Mitchell's story ends. His ashes were buried in a corner of the cemetery, and among the mourners was Helen Cruickshank, whose volume of poems, published under the title *Up the Noran Water*, had won Mitchell's admiration. 'Ponnage', he said, was his favourite. She wrote about that cold, bright afternoon, when a sprinkle of snow lay on the hilltops and the land above the Bervie Water lay red under the spring sun. Farming folk from all over the Mearns had come to Arbuthnott to see Leslie Mitchell's ashes buried. She wondered if they and their kind would ever understand him as he had understood them.

CHAPTER TWO
Painters and Puffins

The village of Catterline sits on top of the cliffs like a topsy-turvy toy-town. From across the bay on the north side of the village, the houses in the South Row seem to be lurching drunkenly downhill towards the door of the Creel Inn, where a steep, narrow road to the harbour divides the village in two. Built on a sloping cliff ridge, the Row and its tilting rooftops mark the line of a street that runs along the rim of a 200 foot drop. Nobody seems to mind. Children play at their front doors, toys are left scattered at the cliff edge, and boats lie upside down on the grass – a long way from the shore below.

The Southsiders shrug off the idea that the cliffs are dangerous. They talk about them as the Braes – and nobody, they say, has gone over the edge yet. 'They're not really cliffs,' said Lil Neilson, a local artist, who lives at No. 2. 'Cliffs ... ' and she jabbed her finger downwards ... 'always go straight down.' They seemed sheer enough to me, but perhaps the folk who live in Catterline have the sort of stoicism that made life bearable for earlier generations of cliff-top dwellers on the Mearns coast.

There were a number of these 'heugh-heid' (cliff-head) fishing villages at one time, but most of them have gone, or have ceased to be fishing communities. Two miles south of Catterline, behind the historic kirk of Kinneff, a narrow footpath leads to a cluster of ruined cottages on top of the cliffs. This is all that is left of the small but prosperous fishing village of Shieldhill, which had twelve fishermen operating from it in the middle of last century. Their boats – five of them – lay in a tiny cove reached by a path that dropped almost precipitously to the shore. In Braidon Bay, next door to Catterline, there was a fishing station called Gapul, or Gaphill, which had two boats catching white fish. It has long since disappeared.

13

Catterline, with its old fisher houses perched high above the half-moon curve of the bay, had two boats operating in 1799. Towards the end of the 19th century, twelve yawls were going to the line fishing, while every summer eight boats set off for the herring fishing. In the *Statistical Account of Scotland* a forward-looking cleric, the Rev. Patrick Stewart, suggested that some money should be 'laid out in raising a small pier at this town'.

A pier was eventually built by Viscount Arbuthnott, who owned the Catterline estate, but the estate changed hands and part of it was bought by an Englishwoman, Mrs Leah Peacock, who first saw the cliff-top village from the sea while sailing up the coast on a north-bound Orkney boat. She was so attracted to it that she decided to live there. After the war, she gave the pier to the fishermen of Catterline in memory of her son, who was killed in the bombing of London. He was an artist, who had often painted beside the pier.

It was in 1950 that another painter, Joan Eardley, first saw that stubby little pier sticking out into the bay. It was to feature in many of her paintings, but neither she nor anyone else could have guessed that Catterline would play such an important part in her life, or that it would so completely absorb her. The old pier, the slanting chimney pots, the fishing nets hanging up to dry, the awesome surge of waves on the rocks ... they were to fill her canvases in the years ahead. It was here that she was to build a reputation as one of the leading landscape painters of her time. More than that, she was to put the little village of Catterline on the map.

The cottages in the South Row, Nos. 1 to 10, are the oldest in the village. Beyond the Creel Inn are the coastguard houses, including the Captain's House, where Mrs Peacock lived. Farther on, another group of old houses completes the semi-circle, while a narrow cliff path goes on to the Watch House, a look-out post in the old smuggling days. Annette Stephen, a well-known Catterline painter, lived in the house with the blue door, No. 21, until her death this year (1991). It was Annette who first introduced Joan Eardley to Catterline. She was Annette Roper then, an art teacher in Aberdeen, living in Stonehaven. Later, she married a Catterline fisherman, Jim Stephen, who died thirteen years ago. His people had fished at Catterline for generations.

Only a few months before her death I sat in her cliff-top cottage and talked with her about her life in Catterline, about the Eardley years, the changes that had taken place (Annette bought her cottage for £40 and today you will pay £75,000 for a house in the village), and about how this tiny Mearns fishing village had cast its spell over her. She fretted about the changes that had taken place, and worried about a painting of the Row that someone had asked her to do – she hated painting to order. She was in her eightieth year then, as nimble as someone half her age, and she was still painting.

One of her water-colours, a road in Mull, hung over her fireplace, full of light and colour. There were two paintings by Lil Neilson, one showing the Row with its sloping rooftops, the other a large oil, 'The Nets.' Given to Annette about fifteen years ago, it captured a part of Catterline that has gone for ever. Not far from it a wood carving of a fish hung on the wall, one eye glaring balefully across the room.

A striking Eardley oil painting of the bay, the pier and the Watch House hung from another wall. Joan Eardley often used old or discarded canvasses to stuff into draughty corners in the roof of her cottage. They were usually paintings that had been thrown aside because she didn't like the way they were shaping. After her death, many of them were taken away by people who wanted one of her works, no matter how good or bad it was, but Annette was unhappy that this was happening to paintings that had been discarded.

Then she herself was offered a huge, incomplete painting on hardboard, one end of which showed the bay from the South Row. It had been used as a draught excluder, and she took it and cut it into strips with the intention of throwing it out. Her agent, who saw the last strip of hardboard lying in Annette's house, asked if he could take it away and repair it. When it came back it had been turned into a complete Eardley painting, restored and framed.

Annette once told me that she had a feeling of guilt about how she acquired the painting, but no one deserved it more, for it was through her that Eardley discovered the Catterline coast in 1950. Annette was looking for a gallery in Aberdeen ('In those days you had to be dead before you could be hung in the Art Gallery') and she was able to get space in a newly-opened exhibition room in the old Gaumont Cinema in Union Street. Searching for something to follow an exhibition of child art at the Gaumont, she heard of a promising painter who had just returned from Italy and France, where she had been on a travelling scholarship. Her name was Joan Eardley.

During the Gaumont exhibition, Annette took Joan to her parents' home outside Stonehaven, but her visitor stayed longer than intended – she fell ill with mumps. It was during her convalescence that she went to Catterline with Annette and was captivated by the clifftop village. Later, returning on holiday, she stayed at the Creel Inn, but before she left she told Annette, 'I think I've found a studio.' It was the old Watch House, standing empty and neglected on the edge of a cliff overlooking Catterline bay. No one had lived there for six years. She could have had the building for £40, but even that small sum was beyond her means. Instead, Annette and her husband bought it, giving Eardley free access to it. While Joan set up her easel in the Watch House, Annette 'took over the cliff'.

When we walked along the narrow cliff path to the old Watch House, Annette pointed out a fishing bothy at the foot of the cliff. At one time, fishermen from other parts of the coast slept in the bothy when they had to go out from Catterline in the early hours of the morning. They passed the time cultivating little gardens outside the bothy. Someone suggested that vegetables should be planted on top of a huge flat-topped rock that lay just off-shore. Grass grew on it, and still does, but what else sprouted on its rocky pate no one now knows. The story is that they tried to turn it into a kailyard. The rock, which featured in many of Eardley's paintings, is still known today as the Kail Tap.

Nothing is left of the fishermen's gardens, but up on top of the cliff another tiny garden grows. This is what Annette

Stephen meant when she spoke about 'taking over the cliff'. She turned the clifftop area around the Watch House into a wild garden, smothering the old building with flowers and bushes. Ripe red 'toms' and fat bunches of grapes grew in a makeshift greenhouse, and in September Red Admiral butterflies fluttered down and painted their own colourful patterns across the garden. From it, Annette could watch seals sunning themselves on the rocks out in the bay (she counted 150 in one year) and below the Watch House was the 'slochy' – a hollow in the rocks – where she kept small lobster pots made for her by her husband.

The Watch House was build about 1750. Holes in the stonework of the window show where there were iron bars. Smugglers and Excisemen played an endless cat-and-mouse game with each other along this stretch of the Mearns coast. Inside the Watch House, the only warlike object was a wooden sculpture of a Viking longboat. Annette called it her 'Spreath'. When an easterly wind blew, throwing up flotsam and jetsam on the shore, her husband, Jim, would say,'Let's go spreathing.' The word 'spreath' means plunder – a raid – and the wood that Annette turned into a Viking longboat was found during a spreathing expedition.

In one room of the Watch House she kept her paintings – and chopped wood. Beyond that was her actual studio, its window looking out over the bay, and at the end of the house was her potting shed, which doubled up as a bedroom in the days when she spent her week-ends at Catterline. The corrugated roof in the potting shed was leaking, but with a touch of ingenuity she had fixed a large piece of plastic under the leak, held up by a clothes peg, so that the rainwater dripped down into a barrel to give her a water supply. The Watch House was Annette's hideout. She was up and away to it in the morning while most people were still in their beds, for that was when the light was best.

Down on the shore a huge piece of hardboard, wrapped in blue plastic, lay against the wall of the fishing bothy. It was a painting by Lil Nellson. Beside it was a small 'cairtie,' a reminder of the days when Joan Eardley pushed her painting materials around Catterline in an old pram. The Makkin' Green, where the fishermen made their nets, was nearby. It was on the Makkin' Green that Eardley did much of her painting, particulary her seascapes. Here, battered by the winds that howled in across the bay, she weighed down her easel with heavy stones to keep her eight-feet long painting boards in place. On one occasion she used an anchor to hold the easel down. She painted as if the sea possessed her – 'black sea, bright green striped sea, brown sea, yellow sea and no sea'. She was dazzled by its changing colours. 'The sea is all whiteness,' she wrote after one fierce storm, 'right far out over the bay, and the bay all thick yellow foam.'

The gales, the blizzards, the unending turmoil of the sea . . . they have a catharetic effect on artists who paint the winter face of Catterline. Joan Eardley once said, 'You really need to be tough for this game.' She wrote about setting up her easel in the teeth of a gale. She tried it three or four times and gave it up because of the length of time left to paint – 'about a quarter of an hour before the onset of the next blizzard'.

Her winter paintings show the Mearns village as few outsiders see it. One of them, *Catterline in Winter*, was painted in the bitter January of 1963, the year that she died. She was living in No. 18 at the time. Her easel seems to have been set on the path between No. 18 and the Creel Inn, so that she was looking across the curve of the cliffs to where the cottages in the Row huddled desolately above the Braes. A pale winter sun struggles hopelessly against a grey, uncompromising sky. There is no sign of life in this bleak landscape. 'The village was like a dead village,' wrote Eardley, during one storm, 'not a soul to be seen.' She thought that staying inside in such weather was 'like giving in to the bullying of the elements'.

In *Catterline in Winter* and in another landscape, *Snow*, the downhill 'slide' of the South Row cottages is clearly shown. Catterline's artists have frequently accentuated this architectural quirk, and now it has become a Catterline image. You see it more acutely from certain viewpoints; from the drying green near the Watch House, and from the road that runs into the village from Crawton. While modern houses on the north side eat into the character of the village, the Row is a reminder that Catterline must never abdicate its past.

No. 1 is the South Row's 'flagship'. It stands on the highest point of the ridge as if leading the crooked little houses towards a new Jerusalem; or, at any rate, away from the encroachment of modern housing development. In 1974, when there were plans to build houses on the Reath, the site of old fortifications behind the Row, the villagers went to the Creel Inn and took down an Eardley painting that had been gifted to the village by Joan's mother. They carried it to the public inquiry to show the heritage they wanted to preserve, and they won their case.

It was in No. 1 that Annette's husband, Jim, was born, and it was there that Joan Eardley set up her studio when she moved to a place of her own in the Row in 1954. There was no electricity, no sanitation, and no water (she had to carry pails of water up the brae every day) but to her it was 'a great wee house'. When I was in Lil Neilson's cottage at No. 2, I thought of Joan Eardley sitting in the room next door, 'looking out at the darkness and the sea', telling herself that she could paint there.

Up on that wind-tormented clifftop, watching the sea pounding the jagged rocks below, Eardley felt a curious sense of wonder. 'This is a strange place,' she wrote. 'It always excites me.' It was not surprising, for this is one of Nature's amphitheatres, where you can sit on top of the world and watch the seasons change, see them come and go, often violently, sometimes with an almost stealthy softness. It wasn't only the sea that attracted her; behind the Row, Eardley painted the land, rich with wild flowers and ripening corn, the fields dipping and diving over the Reath to the muttering tides of Braidon Bay. Lil Neilson, sitting inside her cottage, pointed to the window and said to me, 'Your eye always goes outside. You're always drawn to what's out there.'

Lil bought No. 2 twenty years ago. She first came to Catterline when she had finished her art studies and didn't know what to do with her future. Joan, who by that time had bought No. 18 (she kept No. 1 as a studio and a store), told her to go and live and paint there until she worked things out. When she moved

19

into No. 2 it was an echo of Eardley's earlier experience: an earth floor, no electicity, no water (she had to wait till 1980 for the water), and uninvited guests – owls and rats. There was only one other householder in the Row – Lizzie Melvin (Mrs Taylor), who was called the Mistress by Lil and Annette because of her old-fashioned use of the word 'mistress.' She was a great character, full of stories about Catterline and its folk.

Today, the Creel Inn is run by two Englishwomen, and what Vine Masson would have said about that is anybody's guess. She was a former owner of the Creel who was very much a 'character.' She would sometimes greet unexpected visitors by sticking her head round the curtains of her box bed to say 'hello.' Annette's husband, Jim Stephen, came home on leave from the Navy during the war and went down to the Creel with a mate for a dram. Whisky was rationed in those days and Vine's response was emphatic. 'Na! na!'she said, 'I'm keepin' that for mysel', I've only got one bottle.' They say there are no characters left in Catterline today; perhaps Annette was the last one.

Joan Eardley's painting still hangs in the Creel – 'Given to the people of Catterline by the mother and sister of the artist 1964'. There was talk of taking it down again when new houses were being planned for the north side of the village, but, unlike the fight for the Reath, this was a battle they were bound to lose. The villagers argued that the houses should not be built on top of the cliff, but the local authority said that householders who came to live there should have the same view that others had. So the houses were built – with their backs to the sea.

It is nearly thirty years since Joan Eardley died and her ashes were scattered on the shore at Catterline. So much has changed since then. Lil Neilson believes that the village has been ruined by developments in recent years. She compares it to St Ives and its artists' colony – 'such a pretty place.' She blames 'media hype' for what has happened to it. For all that, it is unlikely that she will move away from Catterline, for she left once before and was drawn back to it. Annette Stephen lived there for nearly forty years, and her love of the place never diminished. 'It's beautiful, especially the sea,' she said. Always the sea.

Only a few days after her death I saw two of the last Catterline canvasses she had painted. They were in the Gallery Heinzel in Aberdeen, one looking across the bay from the path outside the Watch House, with the roofs of the Row standing out against the skyline. The second was called *Storm Seas, Catterline*, a raw, powerful work in which an angry sea filled the canvas. This was the 'black sea, brown sea, yellow sea' of Eardley's vision, for Annette Stephen was as fascinated by these savage waters as her famous contemporary had been when she anchored her easel with stones on the Makkin' Green so many years before.

It was in winter that Annette loved Catterline most ... in the gale-wracked days when sea-spray soared high above the cliffs and sea-weed, tossed into the air by the wind and waves, dropped like sodden streamers in the field behind the Watch House. She once tried to put into words the emotions that the sea aroused in her, but in the end she gave it up, shaking her head and saying simply, 'It's just such a force.'

Annette Stephen's death broke another link with the Eardley era, but she herself added her own chapter to the Catterline story. The last time I saw her she was vanishing along the cliff path to the Watch House, while down on the shore the waves were throwing spray and spume against the Kail Tap. I still remember her final comment on this higgeldy-piggeldy village on top of the cliffs. 'It *does* knock you squint,' she said. No one could argue with that.

About a mile north of Catterline, along a narrow right-of-way path that has almost disappeared, life is slowly coming back to another 'heugh-heid' village. Unlike Catterline, its sister village, Crawton, simply withered away. When the last resident packed his belongings and left in 1927, he closed a history of settlement going back many centuries. In the middle of last century there were twenty-three houses and a school in Crawton. Up to thirty fishermen operated twelve boats, but there was no harbour, only a natural pier-like rock. The path runs down to a shingly beach that lies under near-perpendicular cliffs. Now, after years of dereliction, new houses have been built on top of the cliffs.

This is the land of coutters, queets and Tammy Norries. Their problem is over-population, not de-population, for Crawton is on the doorstep of Fowlsheugh, one of the largest seabird colonies on the mainland of Britain. If ever a place lived up to its name it is Fowlsheugh, where well over 150,000 birds are present and breeding on the Crawton heughs from March to July. The statistics are staggering – 52,000 pairs of guillemots (queets), 4,500 pairs of razorbills (coutters), and 22,000 pairs of kittywakes. There are smaller colonies of herring gulls (300 pairs) and fulmars (300 pairs), with a number of shags resting in caves at the foot of the cliffs. Eiders can be seen on the water, just off shore, while up in their burrows on top of the cliffs there are about 100 pairs of comical Tammy Norries – puffins.

Fowlsheugh was bought as a Reserve by the Royal Society for the Prevention of Cruelty to Birds in 1975. If the noise doesn't lead you to it, the stench will. At the height of the season the sky is alive with birds ... and the air is full of their unending clamour. There were salmon nets below Fowlsheugh at one time, but fishing was banned at the end of last century because thousands of birds were drowned or hanged when they became tangled up in the nets.

The best way to see the colony is by boat. I made the trip from Stonehaven on the *Kia-ora*, which the owner, Ken Singer, described as a kind of modern Fifie. Ken, an electrician, built it himself nine years ago, helped by his brother David. The name, he said, was Maori and meant 'Good Luck.' Grey skies and the threat of rain kept people away on the day I was there, but eight people came on board, settling themselves on old fish boxes. We left Stonehaven, rounded Downie Point and sailed south, past Dunnicaer and the De'il's Kettle to where Dunnottar Castle could be seen brooding on its great rock. The view from the sea gives it a different, majestic perspective.

This harsh, unwelcoming coast is scarred with tunnels, caves and subterranean passages, the most remarkable being the Lang Gallery, some 200 yards long, 40ft. in height and 30ft. wide. They say that small boats can sail through it easily enough. The farther south we went the more birds there were, guillemots and razorbills skimming over the water, puffins scrambling away in a frantic effort to get into the air, their bright beaks bobbing up and down like beacons. Ken Singer moved the *Kia-ora* closer to the cliffs, which were pitted with holes that were readymade nesting sites. As we poked inquisitively into some of the caves, I began to hope that the name of the boat did mean 'Good luck.'

Finally, we broke clear of the cliffs. Todhead Lighthouse could be seen to the south, and as we moved away we caught a glimpse of the roofs of the four houses being built at Crawton. Crawton Bay came into view. Ken pointed out the ridges of rock – the 'slochies,' he called them – which formed piers from the natural rock. From there the fishermen hauled their boats up on to the sand. 'They took boats bigger than mine,' said Ken.

The sky had darkened as we lay off Crawton, and it began to rain. We swung away from the bay and its 'slochies' and headed north to where a band of light was spreading across the horizon at Aberdeen.

CHAPTER THREE
The Torry Coo

Aberdeen folk called it the *Torry Coo*. Its long, melancholy bellow could be heard clear across the city on a damp and foggy night. It stood on the rocks below Girdleness Lighthouse, not far from eight acres of land where the first keepers grazed their cattle more than a century and a half ago. These were *real* cows, but the Torry Coo was the Girdleness foghorn, whose 'voice' was as familiar as the chiming of the Town House clock. It was a gloomy sound, full of foreboding — 'that eerie soun' was how Lillianne Grant Rich described it in her poem 'Foghorn in the Night'. She saw it 'caain a steely knife' into the anxious hearts of people at home. In a sense, her verse was a lament for the passing of the Torry Coo, for in 1987 its voice was silenced for ever. Some people regretted it, but the truth was that there was no place for it in the modern world. Bill Rosie, the last principal keeper at Girdleness, said it was never very effective. Ships were unable to fix the position of the foghorn merely by its sound.

The Torry Coo was a victim of new technology. In 1991, the lighthouse itself suffered the same fate when it was turned into an automatic station. Girdleness, whose light flashed twice every 20 seconds, sent out 200,000 candlepower beams which could be seen 25 miles out to sea on a good night. Today, it is all done by satellite navigation, with computer power instead of candlepower. The fact is that lighthouses are going out of fashion. By the end of this century, Girdleness will probably be no more than a tourist attraction, offering high-level views of the sea and city from its 131-foot tower.

The lighthouse has always had a special place in the affections of Aberdonians. It is the first thing they see when they come clattering out of the railway cuttings at Cove on a train taking them home to the Granite City. John R. Allan, recalling his time in exile, said that he 'sat under the magnolia tree in the scented noon and gasped for a south-east wind off Girdleness.' Alexander Scott wrote about how the 'lichthous plays the lamp-post owre a close', and at week-ends between the wars the Bay of Nigg became the city's playground. Gathering dulse was a favourite pastime. 'We're a' awa' tae Torry rocks tae gither dulse an' tangles' went the lines of an old song.

The curiously-named Brigg of ae Hair was popular with week-end trippers. A brigg is a long, low ridge of rock and the Brigg of ae Hair linked the shore with a cliff called Doonies Craig, just south of Greg Ness, where May Day revellers used to gather. The words 'ae hair', one hair, were used to describe the narrowness of the neck of rock, which was more or less obliterated by rubbish dumped on it when the railway cutting was being made. According to one eighteenth-century report, people went 'over a narrow pass, The Brigg of ae Hair, to Downy-hill, a green island in the sea, where young people cut their favourites' names in the sward'.

Sadly, no young gallants cut their lovers' names on Doonies green island to-day. The whole area has a drab, dejected look about it, despite the fact that it is officially called Loirston Country Park, embracing Kincorth Hill, Tullos Hill, Nigg Bay and the cliff walk south to Cove. The grassland encircling the ruins of old St Fittick's Kirk has become a site for tinkers' caravans, while farther south Tullos Hill is hemmed in by the sprawling ugliness of the Altens industrial estate. Four great burial cairns are lost in a wasteland of gorse and scrub — Cat's Cairn, Crab's Cairn, Tullos Cairn and Baron's Cairn, where beacon fires once blazed to warn the City Fathers that enemy ships were approaching. Now, a rubbish dump smokes and smoulders on the hill. It is a depressing sight. Aberdeen Urban Wildlife Group say the dump is ruining the heathlands of Tullos.

Nevertheless, there are still some playground areas. Walker Park, where the lighthouse keepers grazed their cattle, is a sports field, and behind it are the fairways of Balnagask golf course. Not far from the lighthouse is the old Torry Battery, looking across the wide sweep of Aberdeen Bay. The Battery's guns have rarely been fired in anger. They banged away at two unidentified ships in 1941, but they turned out to be friendly. Below the battery is Greyhope Bay, where a whaler called the *Oscar* went down in 1813. It was after that disaster that Aberdeen's shipmaster asked for a light to be established at Girdle Ness, but twenty years passed before the present lighthouse was built.

Girdleness, rising high above the navigation channel, has seen 150 years of change and progress pass under its winking eye. The whalers and clippers, the little boats, the herring drifters, the face-blackened coal boats, the North boats, the traders and coasters ... they have come riding up that choppy waterway in an endless procession, bobbing a curtsy to Fittie as they headed out for the open sea. The great *Thermopylae* ploughed its way up the channel, and the grubby little *Toiler*, forerunner of what was to become a mighty trawling fleet. Now, with the fleet virtually wiped out, the oil boats have taken over, squat and ugly, butting their way out of the years of slump, back to a second boom. Oil, it seems, is here to stay.

From the lighthouse platform, you can look out across the city's rooftops to the granite heart of Aberdeen and ponder on the fact that it was from the windy acres of Nigg, as well as from Rubislaw, that the Granite City got its nickname. Even the streets of London were paved with 'cassies' from Nigg. Granite quarries were opened at Nigg in 1766, not many years after work began at Rubislaw Quarry, and at one time 600 men were employed there, although the figure dropped drastically to about seventeen by 1772. Some 3,000 tons of stones were exported annually to London, Maidstone, Ramsgate, and other places.

But it was from fishing, not granite, that people in the Nigg and Torry areas made their living. Fiercely-independent little Torry had six boats and thirty-six men engaged in white fishing in 1793, as well as a number of yawls. It also supplied pilots for the port; now, two centuries later, the pilot boats are across the water in Fittie and the old fishing village of Torry has disappeared under a welter of oil tanks. Cove Bay, less than two miles from Gregness, had four boats, with twenty-four men. Aberdeen's home-grown comedian, Harry Gordon, the Laird of

Inversnecky, used to sing about how he rode to Cove on his bike. The air was so strong, he said, that you only needed 'one guff tae feel ye've had enough'. But Aberdonians liked Cove; it was their *Costa del Sol* in the years between the wars, even if the air *was* a bit nippy.

Cove is one of a string of villages clinging limpet-like to the ragged coastline south of Girdleness. In bygone days, the little fishing boats went out to sea before dawn to lay their nets. Women loaded their creels and carried their fish to the market in Aberdeen, while youngsters gathered mussels or lug-worm to bait the next day's lines. It was a hard, unchanging ritual — 'Mony a week oor een never sleekit (shut) on a pillow,' said one fisher-wife. The women would start from Findon 'wi' a birn (load) that took twa tae lift, at three o'clock on a winter's morning, wi' the blin' drift i' the face, and tramp tae Aberdeen by the Brig o' Dee road.' The tangles on their frozen petticoats cut and bloodied their legs as they climbed up 'the lang steep Finnan braes'.

But as the city's fleet expanded many families in the coastal villages pulled up their roots and headed for Aberdeen. The old fishing communities began to die off and with the passing of time a different breed of villagers took their place. They wore grey suits instead of ganzies, and they drove down the 'Steenie' road in fast, expensive cars. They were the new commuters, spreading out from the city like an unstoppable tide. From Girdleness to Dunnottar there were more 'white sarks' than Lewis Grassic Gibbon ever dreamed of when he wrote about Stonehaven's poverty-toffs.

There were a dozen fishing settlements in that 12-mile stretch of coast at one time, including Fittie and Torry. The oldest was at Elsick in Kincardine, but it was abandoned in the eighteenth century. Two once-prosperous settlements, Altens and Burnbanks, both lying between Girdleness and Cove, were abandoned about 1838, partly because of bad harbour facilities.

The coming of the railway in 1849 was the final blow. The sight of fishwives making their daily journey on foot to the city became a thing of the past, although in some cases rail transport actually helped them to extend their markets. The Great North of Scotland Railway had special fish-wife concession fares which allowed them to carry their creels to more distant centres.

The stream of traffic going down the Cove road from Girdleness passes through Burnbanks, where at one time there were twenty thatched cottages, all occupied by fishermen. They had earthen floors and two rooms with a closet in between. Only a handful remain, but the local authority plan to develop the site, so life may yet return to this old Kincardine fishing village. In a sense it already has, for across the railway track, on the edge of the cliffs, I found myself looking down on a cobble that had been hauled up on the shingle at Burnbanks Haven.

A Lossiemouth salmon company had bought the salmon fishing at Altens and Burnbank, as well as at Blackdog, north of Aberdeen, and this was their first season. Bill Childs, the foreman, told me that the boat had come in by sea, while the gear had been lowered down the cliff by winch. Looking at the lone cobble drawn up in that tiny cove, it was hard to believe that four clinker-built yawls once operated from it. The boats were built at Cove and the sails were made at Portlethen, a few miles down the coast.

Portlethen and neighbouring Findon had eighteen boats between them, but Findon itself was of no great importance as a fishing station, largely because there was a lack of proper shelter for its boats. Yet it was better known than many of the larger fishing communities in the North-east, or, for that matter, in Scotland — and all because of its 'Finnan haddies'. Less than a mile from Findon there is a headland with the curious name of Blowup Nose. How it got the name is anyone's guess (it certainly *looks* like a nose), but nothing could be more appropriate for little Findon. A century ago, travellers going along this stretch of Kincardine coast must have sniffed the air in astonishment as they breathed in the smell of burning peat, scorched wood chips and smoked haddock, mixed in with the less pleasant aroma of 'smelly mussel middens'. The fishermen's wives dumped their empty mussel shells in the middens after baiting the lines for their husband's boats. From every 'lum' in the village came the pungent smell of peat smoke and 'haddies'.

Whatever the odour, Findon never wrinkled its nose at it, for it was the humble haddock that put the village on the map. It was like one enormous fish factory, 'finnan haddies' pouring out of it to satisfy an almost insatiable market. There were no smoke kilns in those early days. The fish was smoked over peat and wood chips in wooden kitchen 'lums'. When people tried to get into a house they were often 'smoo'ed oot,' smothered with smoke, and there were times when they had to go down on their hands and knees on the earthen floor to get under it.

Later, there were smoke houses, low, black-tarred sheds with tall wide chimneys built next to the dwelling houses. Dozens of fish, all neatly skewered, were placed in the wide open hearths and cured over slow-burning peats. This succulent sea fare was so popular that the railway authorities had to lay on a special train to carry the fish to Aberdeen — 'oor ain trainie' the Findon folk called it. It came puffing into Portlethen station every Friday to pick up the 'haddies'. Why Findon haddocks were so popular is a mystery, for other fishing villages smoked their fish in the same way. It may have been because Findon was the first village to go in for this type of curing. Ironically, 'finnan haddies' were being sold long after the last fisherman had landed the last haddock at Findon, and some of these so-called Findon fish were trawled by boats from Aberdeen. The final twist to the finnan haddie's tail came when fish-wives from other villages started selling 'finnan' haddocks in Findon itself.

Like whisky-making, the secret of success may have lain in the peat. One reason for the closing down of the Altenshaven fishing station was the lack of good turf and moss for curing haddocks. Peat for the smoking of Findon haddocks was brought home from the Portlethen moss in creels or in barrows without sides. Fibrous sods cut from the top layers were used, for black peat was considered unsuitable. Only good fresh haddock were smoked. It required a greater degree of skill to smoke poor quality fish. During the smoking, the womenfolk sat by the fire and threw sawdust on to the peats.

Fishing died out at Findon in the mid-1920s. Its decline began in the 1870s, the final blow being the introduction of factory acts that made it mandatory to market only 'Findon haddocks' that had been smoked in modern fish houses under strict rules of hygiene. There was a little cottage in Findon, with a fine view of the sea, which was known as Drottie's Hoose. 'Drottie' was the village's last haddock fisherman. To-day, there is nothing left to stir nostalgic memories of the days of the Finnan haddie, no peat reek, no plaque on Drottie's Hoosie, no smelly midden heaps, no tarry smoke houses; only a street called Old Inn Road. The trouble is that no-one knows when there was an inn, or where it stood. The past has disappeared down Findon's throat like a 'haddie' down a hungry man's belly.

The village of Downies, two miles south of Findon, is one of the few villages that still retains a flavour of the past. Here, the fisherfolk also made their living from smoked haddock, but, oddly enough, the fishers themselves never ate the 'haddies'. Jackie Wood, whose father was a fisherman, remembers his mother smoking haddocks, but says that he only got a 'haddie' if one had fallen into the fire. The main food for the fisher families was salt fish — herring and cod. The Woods were real Doonies people, I was told. Jackie lives at No. 18 and the smoke house was where the garage is now. His mother, who sold their fish in the Green at Aberdeen, kept hens, while his father grew potatoes in a cliff-top garden.

Downies is a typical 'heugh-heid' village. Its main street ends in a grassy track which seems to plunge over the edge of the cliff into the sea. Its harbour, like so many others, is incredibly small. Standing on top of the cliff, looking down to the shore, I was thinking of Auld Birsie. He was a Downies fisherman who was immortalised by Aberdeen's pioneer photographer George Washington Wilson. Wilson's photograph showed the grizzled old sea dog wearing a fisherman's woollen cap and smoking a 'cutty' — a short clay pipe complete with metal top and chain. Auld Birsie's real name was George Knowles. Born in Downies, he moved to Stonehaven, where three of his grandchildren still live.

Whatever changes take place in Downies, its story will never be lost. Norman Nicoll and his wife, who live at The Bungalow, have made sure of that. Since they came there thirty-six years ago they have been recording the history of the village. Norman has built up a folio of pictures showing the old Downies alongside the modern village. Meanwhile, Mrs Nicoll has amassed a vast amount of information about Downies and its fisher folk, about people like Moses Wood, Doonies Johnnie, Dod's Meg and Aggie Leiper, who lived to be 100, and about the children, their family names, and the houses, which had lime-washed walls and white wood doors. She has peered into the past to find out how the fisher folk dressed — the men always had flannel next to their skin, including thick flannel drawers, and blue serge surcoats; the women wore white cotton chemises (no drawers of any kind), stays and flannel petticoats. No garments were ever taken off inside the houses.

Downies, like all the other villages along the coast, continues to change. There are few members of the old families still living in the community. The in-comers have taken over, many of them oil people. The work that the Nicolls have put into their research is, in a sense, a reaction not only to change but to the authorities' head-in-the-sand attitude to it Norman Nicoll told me that at one time there was a move to get a Preservation Order at Downies, but nothing came of it. Now the powers-that-be say that the village has changed too much, but, as Norman points out, it was they who allowed the change to take place.

The names of two other tiny fishing villages have been pushed into the background over the years. One is Skateraw, which hangs on to its own identity by the thinnest of threads, for in reality it has been gobbled up by Newtonhill. The harbour is deserted and the pier gone, yet in 1855 there were fifty fishermen in Skateraw and a fleet of twenty-six boats, including eleven drifters and fifteen yawls. More than 130 people were employed in the fishing. The beginning of the end came in 1852 when the railway came to this corner of Kincardine. The station was named Newtonhill and little Skateraw was ignored. Now the name no longer appears even on the map.

The other village is Stranathro, which has been absorbed by Muchalls. Like Skateraw, it has virtually lost its original name, although there is a Stranathro Terrace. Stranathro, which become known as Muchalls in the early 1900s, was a prosperious fishing village, but it would never have won any awards for cleanliness. In 1877, it was pictured in one report as 'composed of wretched hovels, built of clay and thatched with straw'. It had no drainage, roads ankle-deep in mud, and dunghills outside its front doors. The dunghills, like Findon's midden heaps, were made up of 'fish offal and other abominations'.

Yet early this century Muchalls was being lauded as the Scarborough of the North — 'an ideal health resort'. With a little publicity, it was said, it could be crowded with holidaymakers, hundreds of tourists descending on it in the summer months. But it never happened. Muchalls remained the quiet little village it has always been. The only change to the old fisher-town was that the cottages were 'improved' by what one planner called 'ill-designed and over-large dormer extensions'. Davie Cameron, who lives in one of the Stranathro cottages, thinks that the extensions have spoiled the cottages, although his own house has one. When his parents lived in it it was a typical fisherman's cottage with a dry lavatory. His garden is on the opposite side of the road. Lying in it is the skeleton of a boat which he intended to reconstruct but never did.

Nature was in a wild mood when it sculpted this part of the Kincardine coast. Some of the most spectacular cliff scenery in Scotland lies along this eastern seaboard. Here, the waves play their unending sea symphony against a backdrop of grotesquely-shaped rocks with names like Dunie Fell, Tillie Tenant and Scart's Craig. A rock called the Brown Jewel gave its name to a public-house in the village. Mrs Sheila Ogilvie and her late husband, Iain, were converting a local stables into a pub in 1974 and wanted to give it a name in keeping with the district. The *pièce de resistance* is the Grim Briggs, two gneiss rocks through which the waves have cut arches 80 ft high by 50 ft wide. Muchalls' answer to the Old Man of Hoy is the Auld Carl, which is often called the Old Man of Muchalls.

Muchalls also has its Gin Shore, whose name is a reminder of the days when a vast amount of smuggling took place along the coast. There is a ghostly link between the Gin Shore and Muchalls Castle, which lies about a mile inland. This 17th century castle, which is noted for its superb plaster ceilings, is said to be haunted by a Green Lady. It also has a secret staircase and a mysterious underground tunnel leading to a cave at the Gin Shore. According to one story the Green Lady is a girl who was drowned while on her way to meet her lover, a gin smuggler. Back in 1896, the *Aberdeen Free Press* came up with another story about the Muchalls cave. It said that long ago a piper had gone into it playing his bagpipes — and had never returned.

According to one report, the smugglers' tunnel at Muchalls was sealed up by Lord Robertson, Lord Justice General of Scotland, who was tenant of Muchalls Castle at the end of the nineteenth century and took a jaundiced view of smuggling activities on his doorstep. To-day, guide books usually describe the passage as 'lost'. Like most local people, Davie Cameron is sceptical about the mysterious tunnel, but he says there *is* a cave — he has been inside it. That was back in the 1930s. There was no sign of any underground passage then, for the cave was completely blocked by huge boulders

This may have been the 'famous cave' mentioned by the *Aberdeen Free Press* in May, 1896. Although it was commonly believed that the cave went underground to Muchalls Castle, the only information the newspaper could get about it from local people was 'mostly vague theory', and the same could be said to-day. The *Free Press* described how two men had set off to explore the cave — 'or, like the piper, return no more'. They found that it was 300 ft long, with the height from the entrance to the top of the rock close on 200 ft, while the width at the entrance was 41 ft. The first part of it was 'a spacious vaulted chamber' 130 ft long, 16 ft wide and from 40 ft to 50 ft high.

'Above the entrance inside,' said the report, 'the roof is covered with three different species of beautiful ferns in full foliage. The next part of the cave for 100 ft is little more than 3 ft wide, in one or two places being only 16 in. The height

33

is from 30 to 40 ft. The last part widens all at once into a splendid apartment 70 ft. long, 10 ft wide, and about 11 ft high, with a floor of beach gravel sand, perfect, pure and uniform. In this part is the stillness of the grave and the gloom is terrible, but with a candle or two it has a fairy-like aspect. The cave is quite dry from end to end; the tide at high water does not come within several feet of the entrance.'

The *Free Press* report described the cave as 'the noted Blackhill's Cave'. There is a Blackhills Farm between Muchalls and Stonehaven. Mrs Georgina Macpherson, who has been there for over fifty years, had heard of the cave but had never heard it called Blackhills Cave. There have been no recent sightings of the Green Lady, and the piper who marched into the cave blowing a last lament on his bagpipes has long been forgotten, but people still talk about another legendary figure — 'Nippy' Adams. He got his nickname because he was fond of a nip — over-fond, as it turned out — and he lived in another Muchalls cave in the years before the war. He was the first of a number of 'cave-men' I was to meet on my journey round the north-east coast.

'Nippy' was dead by the time Mrs Macpherson arrived at Blackhills in 1939, but she heard about him from her mother-in-law. At first, I pictured the old 'down-and-out' sitting in some other cavernous 'apartment' on the Muchalls shore, candles aglow, enjoying the 'fairy-like' atmosphere while knocking back a bottle of Mother's ruin. But 'Nippy's Cave' was a much more modest affair than the Gin Shore cave. It had an old sack over the entrance to shut out the winds that came whistling in over the head of the other 'Auld Carl' at Muchalls. 'Nippy' needed a drop of the hard stuff to keep himself warm, but it was whisky, not gin, that was his downfall. He was often seen making his erratic way from the Gin Shore to the Marine Hotel for his daily sustenance, and to get there he had to cross the main Aberdeen railway line. One night, having taken a nip too many, he was struck by a passing train and killed.

CHAPTER FOUR
The Dracula Trail

Aberdeen Bay curves away from the Don estuary in a great arc of golden sand. Between the sand and the links just north of the river's mouth is a spot known as the Uploup. This was where travellers literally louped or jumped from the sand to the links on their way along the earliest coastal road from Aberdeen to Peterhead. Because it was difficult to find in the dark, two poles were erected at the spot — 'Two poles at the up Loups', read an entry in the Aberdeen Council Register for 10 December 1715.

More than two centuries later, a new coastal trail for walkers is being mapped out, much of it touching the route taken by travellers like Thomas Pennant, the writer and naturalist, who toured Scotland in 1769 and wrote about riding 'for some miles on the sea sands' to Newburgh. Gordon District Council have surveyed the coastal area as far as their boundary with Banff and Buchan. The Banff and Buchan council would like to see a long-distance footpath between Whinnyfold and Cullen, and a link up with Gordon would bring about a much longer coastal trail stretching from Aberdeen to Boddam.

The old coastal road, according to an Act of 1686, went 'from the Bridge of Don (Balgownie) to the said Up-Loup and from the Garbel-head upon Ithen towards the House of Bowans, and thence to Peterhead'. The Garble-Head, or Garpelhead, is at the mouth of the Tarty Burn at Newburgh, where there was a ford and ferry over the River Ythan before the Waterside bridge was built. On the far side was the Sleek of Tarty. The word 'sleek' means mire or mud, and it was across these oozy mudflats that carts once crossed at low tide. From Waterside Farm, on the east bank of the Ythan, they went through what is now the Sands of Forvie Nature Reserve, coming out east of Cotehill Loch before turning down to Collieston.

The House of Bowans or Bowness was Slains Castle, but between Collieston and Cruden Bay there is another castle with the same name — Old Slains Castle. This shattered ruin sticks up like a broken tooth, gaunt and impressive against the Buchan skyline. It sits on a headland called the Bow. Behind it the cliffs drop 120 feet to the sea. Fifty fishermen lived and worked in this clifftop community last century. Julie McCulloch, a comparative newcomer to Old Slains, pointed out that there were only four occupied houses in the village, yet her house was No. 19. She discovered from the title deeds that the ruined house next door had been the local shoppie and that she and her husband were living in the potter's place. They had come north from Glasgow looking for a rural home near Aberdeen, and this was what they were offered — a cottage perched on a rocky headland on the windy sea-edge of Buchan. Most people would have turned up their coat collars and walked away, but the McCullochs stayed.

Julie thought she would have to have a crash course in local history to deal with visitors. She could start by directing them to the Swedish-type timber building at the foot of the ruined castle. Rented out by the Countess of Erroll, it has a great stone crest over the fire with the motto, 'Gang warily'. Outside, in the garage, a plaque reads: 'Built 1664 by Gilbert XI, Earl of Erroll, Great Constable of Scotland'. One American wanted to know where the smugglers' caves were. There is certainly no lack of them in this area. Muchalls had its Gin Cave, but Dick Ingram, an old worthy at Collieston, once told me about a cave there called the Gin Hole, swearing that he would 'get gin oot o' it afore I dee'. I never discovered if he did. Late last century, a writer called James Dalgarno wrote about a ramble on the east coast had pinpointed places like the Blin' Man's Rock at Slains, where Holland gin and brandy were hidden. He went into the Dripping Cave, a dark hole with 'rugged arches and gloomy passages, goblin-like imagery, slimy cells and constant drippings'. Most of these caves are now inaccessible.

Old Slains Castle was blown up by James VI after the ninth Earl of Erroll had joined the Catholic forces opposing him at the Battle of Glenlivet, and the new castle was built to replace it. It was the home of the Earls of Erroll, chiefs of the Clan Hay, for three and a quarter centuries, being rebuilt three times before it was finally abandoned.

The ragged ruins of New Slains Castle lie five miles to the north. This gloomy skeleton of a building has an afinity with James Dalgarno's 'goblin-like imagery', although you are unlikely to see any goblins in this day and age. You may have to settle for a mermaid. Dalgarno wrote about a fisherman called Tammas Robertson, who saw and spoke with a mermaid one misty morning in May, 1836. Peter Buchan, in his *Annals of Peterhead*, said that Buchan seafaring men thought that 'the grottos and chasms of this rocky coast are tenanted with them'. He told the story of a small Peterhead boat that was driven ashore near Slains Castle after a mermaid had climbed on to its bowsprit. Only one man survived.

There are, it has to be said, worse things than mermaids. When the moon rises over the roofless towers of the old castle it can bring out such Gothic horrors as vampires and werewolves. Count Dracula lurks in the ruins, flourishing his cloak like a pair of bats' wings and baring his blood-stained teeth; or, as Bram Stoker pictured him, with bloated flesh and 'gouts of fresh blood' on his lips. When Stoker wrote this gory description of him in *Dracula*, the Count had been out during the night, doing his worst, and when daylight came he was lying 'gorged with blood, like a filthy leech'.

Some people would have you believe that it all happened among the tottering ruins of Slains Castle, or, at anyrate, that the idea of Stoker's horror novel bred like a maggot in his brain while he was staying at Cruden Bay. The cult of vampirism has been growing in this corner of Buchan in recent years — all in the cause of tourism, of course, and the popular assumption is that it was from Slains Castle that Stoker got his inspiration for the novel. It has also been said that he began writing it while staying at Cruden Bay. There was evidence, according to Banff and Buchan Tourist Board, that early drafts of the story had the evil count coming ashore at Slains when he arrived in Britain, and that this was later changed to Whitby in Yorkshire.

So now the Buchan coastal trail has become the Dracula Trail. One official tourist publication even went into detail about the route to follow from the Bullers of Buchan — that 'monstrous cauldron', as James Boswell called it — to Cruden Bay, where Bram Stoker stayed at the Kilmarnock Arms Hotel. From there, it said, the trail went on to the village of Whinnyfold, where he spent his holidays. 'Once again you are following in the footsteps of Dracula', it declared. In fact, you are doing nothing of the sort. Over the years, Slains has become part of the Dracula legend, but it played no part in the creation of Bram Stoker's gory vampire.

Whitby has a Dracula Trail, complete with guide book and a 'Dracula Experience', but Bernard Davies, chairman of the Dracula Society, was taken aback by the suggestion that there might be a similar trail in the north-east of Scotland, despite the fact that the late Sir Ian Moncrieffe of that Ilk was a member of the society, as is his son, the present Earl of Erroll. The society organises Dracula tours to Romania and to sites associated with Vlad the Impaler, on whom Stoker's Dracula was based. A Frankenstein tour was being planned when I spoke to Mr Davies, and also a trip that seemed to me like driving a stake through Dracula's heart — a *sun-seekers'* holiday on a Greek Isle of Vampires. I always thought that vampires disappeared into their coffins when the sun came up.

The Dracula Society has no plans to visit Cruden Bay. The village, says it chairman, is certainly associated with Bram Stoker, but only marginally with Dracula. Yet the legend dies hard. Only a few days before I contacted him at his home in London the same story had been repeated in the *Sunday Times* in an article about the sale of a cottage at Whinnyfold. 'No doubt the locals up at Cruden Bay would like a "Dracula Trail" of their own,' said Mr Davies, 'but I'm sure I don't know what you would put in it. It would be a very short one, to say the least,' adding thoughtfully, 'Twice round the bar of the Kilmarnock Arms is one possibility.'

Bram Stoker first saw Cruden Bay in 1893, during a walking tour of the Buchan coast, but he began his novel *Dracula* much earlier, probably in late 1889, and by early 1890 had written the opening plot and the action at the Count's semi-ruinous castle. Even if he had seen the castle before starting the novel it would have played no part in Dracula's incarnation, for it was anything but ruinous at that time. Rebuilt in 1836, and still the home of the Earls of Erroll, it was occupied long after Bram Stoker had departed, taking his monstrous Count with him. In 1926 it was bought by a Dundee contractor and demolished. The present ruin gives little indication of how it looked in its hey-day, for it was an elegant building, with stepped gables, pepperpot turrets, an outside staircase, and a basement. At the turn of the century it was owned by Sir John Ellerman, the shipping magnate, but he never lived in it; in fact, he never even came north to see it.

Pepperpot turrets were incorporated in another building that put Cruden Bay on the map. This was the Cruden Bay Hotel, built by the Great North of Scotland Railway in 1899 when the railway came to the village. It was the wonder of Buchan, holding out the promise of Cruden Bay becoming the 'Brighton of Aberdeenshire'. In had 140 rooms, red-carpeted staircases, furniture of Chippendale mahogany in Louis XV style, a billiard room, a writing room, and 'every modern comfort', including electric light and a lift. It also had a golf course that is still one of the finest in the north-east.

The folk of Cruden, whose contact with the gentry had been confined to tipping their bonnets to the laird at Slains, looked on the coming of the hotel with a mixture of undiluted awe and furtive speculation, wondering in their canny way how they could profit from it all. Local girls found themselves donning navy-blue *crêpe de chene* dresses, with white caps and stiff collars, before serving up exotic dishes to the wealthy guests. The village coalman, scrubbing his hands clean, unhitched his horse and went off to pull a line of white bathing machines to the beach. From outside the village, fee'd loons from the farms cycled in to join the caddymaster's queue. There could be as many as 100 boys waiting to act as caddies. If they were selected they got 1/3p a round, and, if they were *unlucky*, a kiss from her ladyship at the end of the season. Some of the caddies learned their golf on the Cruden Bay course, whacking away at hackit ba's with old mashies and niblicks.

Up at the railway station, said to be 'one of the most artistic stations on the whole railway', the train from Ellon disgorged a string of millionaires. They were taken to 'the palace on the sandhills' in two electric tramcars, each carrying sixteen passengers. Both were turned into summer houses after the hotel was demolished in 1952, but they were allowed to deteriorate. In 1990, it was decided to cannibalise the worst car to reconstruct at least one version of the Cruden Bay 'trammie'.

The tramcars carried an endless procession of top people to the hotel, tycoons like Sir Jeremiah Colman, the mustard magnate, Sir William Burrell, whose 'Burrell Collection' now draws thousands of art lovers to Glasgow, and families who gave their names to famous brands of wine, cigarettes, beer and biscuits — the Gilbeys, the Wills, the McEwans and the Crawfords. They wined, dined, golfed, fished, played bowls, tennis and croquet, and walked across the sands to take afternoon tea in Whinnyfold. Bram Stoker, who couldn't afford to stay at the Cruden Bay Hotel, often went for a stroll on the sands with his wife, Florence, ending up at the rocks near Whinnyfold, which the locals called Finnyfa' or Finnyfaul. When 'Brammie' was writing, Florence, who was known as Mrs Bram, played golf on the new course. She was said to be one of the prettiest woman who ever walked the Cruden Bay fairways.

The old Whinnyfold was set well back from the cliffs, but to-day the villagers look clear across the bay to the notorious Scaurs of Cruden. The view is spectacular, but for the fishermen who lived there a century ago life was hard and exacting. Back in 1855, there were 58 fishermen in Whinnyfold, compared with 180 in Port Erroll (it was re-named Cruden Bay in 1924). It was among the jumble of cottages in Finnyfa' that Bram Stoker spent many of his holidays. In his novel, *The Mystery of the Sea*, he described it before the Cruden Bay Hotel was built ... 'a few rows of fishermen's cottages, two or three great red-tiled drying sheds in the sand-heap behind the fishers' houses, a little lookout beside a tall flagstaff on the northern cliff, a few scattered farms over the inland prospect, one little hotel down on the western bank of the Water of Cruden.'

Not much has changed. The little hotel was the Kilmarnock Arms in Cruden Bay, where Bram Stoker stayed when he first visited this corner of Buchan. There is still a look-out hut on the Whinnyfold cliffs, but it is in ruins. John George Cay, who has been a fisherman for over sixty years, told me it was the work of vandals. John, who is eighty, lives at No. 12 Whinnyfold, which still boasts a box bed. He is not, strictly speaking, a Finnyfa' man, for before he was born his father left Whinnyfold and went off to the seasonal herring fishing at Peterhead, taking his wife with him, and John was born in the Blue Toon, in the district known as the Queenie. 'They called me a Queenie Arab,' he said.

John was one of the boys in the caddymaster's queue. He remembers caddying for the hotel guests when he was a lad of fourteen. In addition to his 1/3p he sometimes got a shilling tip, at other times only sixpence. On one occasion he was given the handsome sum of two shillings. 'I thought I was made,' he said.

He first shipped aboard a Peterhead drifter in 1927 at the age of sixteen, and he can look back on the days when every house in the village was occupied by a fisherman. Now they are all incomers. One of the houses is called 'The Crookit Lum', but it has less to do with its chimney than with the *Crookit Mary* and the *Crookit Meg*, two luggers heavily involved in the smuggling trade. John's grandfather, who was also a fisherman, lived in 'The Crookit Lum', but it had no fancy name then.

Standing with him on the cliffs, looking down on the tiny cove, I remembered a sketch by the Macduff artist, Peter Anson, showing six or seven boats lying askew on the rocks at Whinnyfold, with cottages nudging each other on the clifftop, the familiar black sheds in front of them. It seemed to me a miracle that *any* boats should sail from there at all, yet Finnyfa' was one of the most enterprising fishing communities in the north-east. In the middle of last century it had a fleet of 24 boats, including three large drifters used for the herring fishing. The fishermen were also known as the most successful great-line fishermen on the east coast of Scotland.

John pointed to a white boat drawn up on the shore. 'That's mine,' he said. But he had hurt his back hauling it out of the water and had begun to think that his fishing days were over. Below us, the waves rolled in, filling up two natural channels or troughs in the rocks — 'trochs' was the Doric word that John used; the south troch and the north troch. They were the equivalent of the 'slochies' I had seen at Crawton in Kincardine. 'If these trochs hadn't been there,' said John. 'Finnayfa' would never have existed.' Bram Stoker mentioned such troughs in *The Mystery of the Sea*. 'Through the masses of rocks that run down to the sea from the sides and shores of all these bays,' he wrote, 'are here and there natural channels with straight edges as though cut on purpose for the taking in of the cobbles belonging to the fisher folk of Whinnyfold.'

From where we stood we could see over the shattered coastguard hut to the Scaurs of Cruden, which have claimed more ships and lives than most people care to count. The names sound out like a roll-call of the doomed — the *Daisy*, the *Chigwell*, the *Hartfell*, the *Malvina*, the *Quaker City*, the *Saracen*, the *City of Oska*, the *Milwaukee*, and many more. There is a certain grim irony in the story of the cargo steamer *Milwaukee*, which ran aground on the Scaurs in September, 1898. A remarkable salvage operation was carried out, but, having survived the Scaurs, the vessel was torpedoed and sunk in August, 1918. The *Milwaukee* ran aground because its captain mistook a flashing light for Buchan Ness Lighthouse. In fact, it was a flare-light being used in the building of an embankment for the Cruden Bay to Boddam railway line.

The American vessel *Quaker City*, which ran aground on the Scaurs in March, 1921, was also taken off the reef, but twenty years later it shared the same fate as the *Milwaukee* in another war. She was torpedoed in the Atlantic in May, 1942. These are the true stories of the dreaded Scaurs, often more dramatic than the legends which have been told about the killer reef. One fanciful tale says that when there is a full moon at the Lammas tide those with the 'sight' can see the bodies of victims claimed by the Scaurs rising out of the sea. Bram Stoker based *The Mystery of the Sea* on this legend, and I told John Cay of how it drew an eerie picture of the sea giving up its dead:

Up the steep path came a silent procession of ghostly figures, so misty of outline that through the grey green of their phantom being the rocks and moonlit sea were apparent, and even the velvet blackness of the shadows of the rocks did not lose their gloom. And yet each figure was defined so accurately that every feature, every particle of dress or accoutrement could be discerned. Even the sparkle of their eyes in that grim waste of ghostly grey was like the lambent flashes of phosphoric light in the foam of moving water cleft by a swift prow. There was no need for me to judge by the historical sequence of their attire, or by any inference of hearing; I knew in my heart that these were the ghosts of the dead who had been drowned in the waters of the Cruden Skares.

'That's some yarn,' said John, disbelievingly.

Fish, not fantasy, was his concern. He had heard Bram Stoker spoken about a lot in his younger days — too much, in fact. 'I couldn't stick hearin' about him,' he said. 'It went in one ear an' out at the other.' To him, reality was more important than 'Brammie's' fanciful tales. His life has been played out against the background of the infamous Scaurs, and they were fearful enough without phantoms and 'phosphoric' lights popping up over Finnyfaul.

One particular wreck held a special poignancy for him. In February, 1903, the Danish steamer *Xenia* struck the Scaurs, sparking off one of the most dramatic rescues seen off the Aberdeenshire coast. John's father was among the Whinnyfold fishermen who launched a boat that terrible night and went to the rescue of the stricken ship. The Port Erroll lifeboat was also called out and John has always resented the fact that the Port Erroll men were given most of the credit for the rescue. When I was with him he was complaining about a magazine article which said that the Port Erroll lifeboat had rescued all but two of the crew. It also reported, incorrectly, that the lifeboatmen's bravery had been recognised by two awards, one from the Danish Government, the other from the British Government. It was, in fact, the Whinnyfold men who got the medals.

In the days when Whinnyfold was a 'fisher toon', and not a retreat for oil men and white collar workers, there was never any love lost between Finnyfa' and Port Erroll. The Port Erroll fishermen, according to a poem which John dug out from a drawer, were always boasting about their superiority. They looked down on their neighbours across the bay:

> They brag to us, Port Erroll folk,
> Their toon wi' oors they widna trock,
> For theirs is founded on a rock
>   At Finnyfaul.

The poem, called 'Whinnyfold,' puts the record straight about the Xenia rescue:

> Wha hisna heard o' that brave band
> Of men that lent a willing hand
> That day the *Xenia* struck the land
>   Near Finnyfaul.
>
> Whilst on the Scaurs the breakers roar,
> They rowed them all, but two, ashore,
> Such valiant deeds they've done an' more
>   At Finnyfaul.

John's father, Alec, and his two uncles are mentioned in the poem — 'There's Alec, Joe and Willie Cay.' There were 25 men on the *Xenia*. The survivors were given shelter in the fishermen's homes in Whinnyfold, and the captain, 'a big fat man', was put up by Bram Stoker's landlady, with the result that she was invited to visit him in Denmark.

'That was my Aunt Isy,' said John.

John didn't know if his Auntie Isy had accepted the captain's invitation, but from all accounts she did go to Copenhagen. She must have been quite a woman, for as well as being landlady to Bram Stoker and looking after her old mother she catered for the hotel guests who strolled across the sands to have afternoon tea at Whinnyfold. During the summer she moved into her wash-house and used her cottage to entertain the visitors. Her baked scones were so popular that she had to take over the houses of relatives who were away to the fishing, using them to set up a series of tea-rooms. It all paid off in the end, for Isy met and married the captain of a ship that had been wrecked on the Scaurs. He returned to Whinnyfold to salvage the vessel — and fell in love with Aunt Isy and her scones.

As well as putting the record straight on the *Xenia* rescue, the Whinnyfold poem painted a vivid picture of life in this Buchan village at the turn of the century. The Whinnyfold of that time was regarded as a 'modern toon', standing 'near the cliff held'. But there was also old Whinnyfold — the 'auld thack toon' — where Mrs Hay served up 'her famed pork pie' and Willie Walker, an invalid who had 'wrocht in's bed for mony a year', made bairns' toys. There were Hays, Freelands, Morgans, Wilsons, Cormacks and M'Phersons — and, said the poet, 'they're a' decent persons at Finnyfaul.' He hoped they would be catching fish at Finnyfa' for a long time to come.

But the tale of auld Finnyfaul had to come to an end. John Cay was the last fisherman to launch his boat, the *Ebenezer*, from the beach at Whinnyfold. It was a symbol of what had happened to fishing in many of the small North-east ports. There is virtually nothing in Port Erroll or Whinnyfold to show that they were once busy fishing communities. Commercial fishing ended in Port Erroll in 1965, although salmon fishing provides work at Cruden Bay throughout the season.

Helicopters clatter across the coast on their way to the oil fields — messengers of change. Down in Cruden Bay the fishing boats have gone, the railway has been dismantled, and the hotel has vanished, but the golf course that brought a steady flow of well-heeled industrialists and their wives to the 'Brighton of Aberdeenshire' has become the gateway to a new kind of wealth — oil. The south end of Cruden Bay golf course is now the landfall of BP's North Sea oil pipeline from the Forties Field. After the pipeline had been laid the fairways were returned to their original condition. No one would have known that anything had changed, but the stamp of oil had been firmly implanted in the soil of Buchan.

Oil, a luxury hotel, a ruined castle said to be haunted by a vampire — that was Cruden Bay's story. I took a last look at the Seal Rock, which John had pointed out, and at the dark ridge of the Scaurs, where the *Xenia* had gone down. 'There are a lot of my lobster pots donwn there,' John had told me. They had been caught in the wreckage and had never come up. As I turned away from Whinnyfold, past the ruins that marked the site of the 'auld thack toon', I looked across the bay and thought of the man who had *first* put Cruden Bay on the map. I could see him tramping across the sands, red-bearded, dressed in tweeds, a beret on his head and a stick in his hand, preoccupied with the ghosts and vampires that peopled — and perhaps plagued — his imagination. Bram Stoker, ill and no longer able to afford the cost of the Kilmarnock Arms, returned to Cruden Bay for the last time. He rented a fisherman's cottage called 'Isie-leay's', overlooking the sea, and spent a month there. He died in London on 20 April, 1912, at the age of sixty-four.

The old kirkyard of Ecclesgreig at St Cyrus. It was here, sitting against the kirkyard wall, that the Montrose lawyer-poet George Beattie shot himself when he was jilted by a local farmer's daughter.

Salmon fishers mend their nets on the sands at St Cyrus. There have been complaints about litter and pollution on the St Cyrus beach yet it is still one of the loveliest beaches In the Northeast of Scotland.

Sand and sea form an intricate pattern on the beach at St Cyrus. Here, the beach is seen from the cliffs near the village. In the foreground are two salmon bothies.

Gourdon Harbour. Alex Welsh's line boat Enterprise is seen berthed between two other vessels.

Alex Welsh baits his hooks in a shed in the back garden of his home at Gourdon, making them ready for the next day's fishing in his line boat *Enterprise*.

Lil Neilson outside her home in the South Row at Catterline.
Below is the pier, which featured in many of Joan Eardley's
paintings, and beyond it is the Makkin' Green, where fishermen
mended their nets. On top of the cliffs is the Watch House.

Annette Stephen in her studio in the Watch House. In front of
her is a painting she was working on, showing the South Row.
The old Watch House lay empty for years until Annette and her
husband, Jim, bought it and gave Joan Eardley access to it.

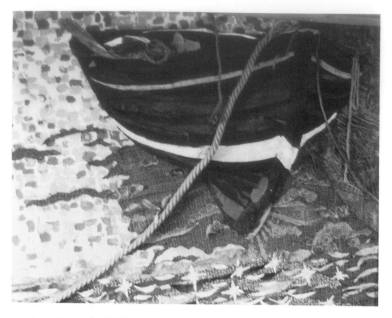

A collage of a fishing boat hung on a wall of the Watch House. Annette Stephen's husband, Jim, was a fisherman and at one time Catterline had twelve yawls going to the line fishing.

The South Row above the Braes of Catterline. It was here that Joan Eardley had a studio, looking out over the bay and across the water to the Watch House, where she also did much of her painting.

The Torry Coo on its rocky seat below Girdleness Lighthouse.

The Torry Coo — the foghorn that once wailed its message across Aberdeen's rooftops. Now the "Coo" is silent and Girdleness Lighthouse has been automated.

An oil supply ship returning from the North Sea oil platforms manoeuvres its way into Aberdeen harbour, passing the North Pier and Round House on its way to its berth.

Davie Cameron and his wife outside their cottage in the old fishertown of Stranathro at Muchalls. It was said by a planner that the cottages had been spoiled by "ill-designed and over large dormer extensions". Davie remembers when his house was a typical fisherman's cottage with a dry lavatory.

There is an eerie look about the ruins of Slains Castle at
Cruden Bay and many people think that Bram Stoker got his
inspiration for 'Dracula' from the building. In fact, the castle
was still standing when Stoker spent his holidays in this part
of Buchan.

The Ythan estuary, where terns breed among the sand dunes.
The area is a well-known haunt of naturalists. Newburgh, on
the shore of the River Ythan, houses Culterty Field station,
where Aberdeen University researchers carry out studies in
ornithology, zoology and biology.

The famous Bullers of Buchan. They were visited by Boswell
and Johnson, who explored the caves and rocks below. From
the tiny village on top of the cliffs a narrow path leads along
the edge of the Bullers.

John Cay above the cliffs at Whinnyfold. Off this part of the Buchan coast are the Scaurs of Cruden, which have claimed many ships over the years.

Whinnyfold, a typical 'heugh-heid' or cliff-top fishing village.
Today most of the houses have been bought by incomers.

Old Slains Castle and the fisher houses in earlier years.

The poet Peter Buchan on the quayside outside his home at
Mount Pleasant. In the background, across the water, is the
Queenie, where the blocked-up windows of old warehouses are
a reminder that they once housed many local people — the
Queenie Arabs. Today the Queenie is completely given over to
oil and industry.

The Cruden Bay Hotel, with the old tramcar at its entrance.

Looking across Peterhead Harbour to Shore Street, an elegant part of the town in the days when it was a popular spa. The house with its gable end to the street is Peter Buchan's home, Mount Pleasant.

Fish boxes pile up, ice spills onto the quayside, and the catches swing from the boats onto the fish market floor. This is an everyday scene at Peterhead Harbour, which is now one of the country's top fishing ports.

Peterhead Harbour crowded with fishing boats ... a sign of the prosperity that has come to the Buchan fishing port in recent years. It is the main landing port for a fleet of about 300 vessels.

Maggie's Hoosie in Shore Street, Inverallochy. There are plans to turn it into a museum, but some local folk are sceptical. They say it just wouldn't be Maggie's Hoosie.

Joe and Jessie Duncan outside their home at Boatlea Cottages. They say that this was where the "lost" village of Boatlea once stood, and that another vanished community, Corsekelly, was nearby.

"Under this ston lyes ... ". This tombstone is one of the gravestones in the kirkyard of St Fergus, which is near the site of the old village of Drumlinie. Today, nothing at all remains of the village; its exact site is unknown.

Kinnaird Head Lighthouse and the Wine Tower near the shore at Fraserburgh. The lighthouse, automated in 1991, is to become a museum, and the Wine Tower, built in the late 16th century as a private chapel, is to be restored.

Jim Oliver, principal keeper at Kinnaird Head lighthouse until it became automatic, looks over the rooftops of Fraserburgh from the lighthouse platform. The Kinnaird light could be seen from a distance of 25 miles, although some old fishermen claimed to have seen its glow from 40 miles away.

The village of Pennan, a North-east village with "one foot in the sea." Pennan's red telephone box put the village on the map when it was used as a location for the film "Local Hero", starring Burt Lancaster.

Pennan seen from Cullykhan Bay.

A Banffshire 'folly' – this curious double-storey bridge spans the Burn of Buckie in the Braes of Enzie. The original lower storey of the bridge was used by pack horses.

This old blacksmith's shop stands in the tiny hamlet of Drybridge in the Braes of Enzie. The smiddy was run by the husband of Mrs Sheila Duncan (seen right outside the building), but when he died two years ago his son Alan (left) turned it into an antique business.

St Gregory's Chapel, Preshome, in the heart of the Enzie farmland. Almost cathedral-like in appearance, it had 1400 names on its list of communicants in 1829.

Nets lie along the quay at Gardenstown, overlooked by the
Church of Scotland kirk on the hill. Gardenstown was once a
Brethren stronghold.

"If the Lord will ... ". The sign can be seen outside a mission hall in a narrow close at Gardenstown. Many of the meeting places of the various religious groups were in the back-streets and closes of the older fisher towns.

The domed clock tower of Macduff's Doune Church dominates
the Banffshire port, but a clock is missing on one side of the
tower. Macduff people built their church with an empty clock
face so that their neighbours in Banff wouldn't be able to
tell the time. The huge ship's anchor beside the church was
dragged up in the nets of a local fishing boat.

Banff's magnificent Duff House. There are plans to turn the
historic building into an outpost of the Scottish National
Gallery, exhibiting paintings appropriate to a country house
of its era.

Jim Merson (left), secretary of the Buckie and District Fishing
Heritage Society, with John ('Bodge') Murray. In their premises
the society are building a picture of what life was like in this
busy fishing community in bygone years.

A model of an old Zulu fishing boat, on display in the Buckie
Heritage Society's showrooms.

The clifftop fishing port of Portknockie. The port was founded
in 1677.

A sea view of Findlater Castle — Banffshire's 'miniature Gibraltar'. This 15th-century fortress clings precariously to the rocks near the village of Sandend.

Findlater Castle from the land.

Fordyce Castle stands in the middle of the quaint, old-fashioned village of Fordyce. Fordyce was the home of George Smith, who made his fortune in Bombay and left money to found a school for the teaching of boys with the name of Smith.

Charlie the hermit outside his cave.

Bob Bruce manoeuvres the *Toby* into Sandend Harbour. On the left is the Muckle Hoose, a former watch house, which is used by Bob as an unorthodox navigation aid when coming into port.

Sandend as it was when it was a busy fishing port. Now it is a popular holiday spot.

Alex Howe and Eric Goodman, with his dog Benny, seen outside the icehouse at Tugnet. The icehouse, once the biggest in Scotland, has been turned into a museum.

Eric Goodman (left) and Angus Gordon, manager of the Tugnet Salmon station, with salmon netted from the River Spey.

The sea laps the entrance to one of the Covesea caves, while in the distance can be seen the tall finger of Covesea Lighthouse.

A grotesque, twisted pillar of rock rises from the shore at
Lossiemouth — one of the curious shapes that nature has
sculpted from the rocks at Covesea.

The lighthouse at Covesea rises over one of the many caves
that can be seen along this stretch of the Moray coast.

Norman Whyte at work on one of the boats in his shipbuilding yard at Findhorn. He builds salmon cobbles, dinghies and pleasure craft for customers all over Britain.

The mysterious Michael Kirk at Gordonstoun, where the Wizard of Gordonstoun is buried. The ancient Kirk of Ogstoun once stood here, and the mediaeval Ogstoun market cross, with its five-pointed cross, is in the middle of the graveyard.

The round square at Gordonstoun School, built by the Wizard, Sir Robert Gordon, in 1690, as a stable-block. It was described as "a scientific sanctuary for his soul". Today it houses classrooms and a library.

Pleasure craft lie in Nairn Harbour, which was at one time a busy fishing port. Now it has only one registered boat, which fishes from other ports.

Margaret Bochel inside the Fishertown Museum at Nairn. The story of the Nairn fishing community is on permanent record in the museum at the Laing Hall, which is visited by over 2000 people each year.

The 16th century beehive doocot near Gordonstoun House, built by 'Ill' Sir Robert Gordon, son of the Wizard of Gordonstoun. It was said that building a doocot brought a death in the family — and 'Ill' Sir Robert wanted rid of his wife.

The 17th-century Leitcheston doocot in the Enzie, south of Portgordon. This crowstepped doocot has four small doo dormers leading into separate doo dormitories.

CHAPTER FIVE
The Buchan Clan

They were the golden years ... the time when a band of bare-footed Peterhead fisher loons went off to explore the secret corners of the Blue Toon. They were only ten or twelve years old, but they knew there must be more to life than buckies and bandies and dank piles of tangle rotting in the summer sun, so they went in search of it. Their wanderings took them to Inverugie, where they found not one castle, but two, their broken walls whispering of long-ago battles, while up on a steep grassy rise was a granite dyke that had 'kirk windows' in it. Looking through them, they could see a garden where there were 'old-fashioned flowers with old-fashioned names', a fairyland of quilted fields, leafless trees and 'frail primroses with timid eyes'. It was easy to see why it was called Mount Pleasant.

One of those barefoot boys was Peter Buchan, the fisher poet of Peterhead, and for him the name Mount Pleasant was to become almost a trademark. He wrote a poem about it — 'that place of pure delight' — and in it he reached back through the years to what he still regards as a golden period of his life. When another Buchan writer, David Toulmin, read the poem he said it brought tears to his eyes. Later, 'Mount Pleasant' became the title of a book of poems about Peterhead and its fisher folk, about the Lazy Dyke and the Queenie, the Pinkie Braes and the Collieburn, and about the pleasure of having a hoosie by the sea 'wi' five-an-twenty ripper codlins dryin' at the door'. It ran into five editions. Now, a lifetime away from those carefree days of his youth, Peter Buchan is seeing out his years in the corner of Peterhead where he was born and brought up. The sights and sounds of the port are on his doorstep — and the name of his house is 'Mount Pleasant'.

It seems as if everybody knows Peter Buchan. His Doric poetry has won him friends far outside Buchan. He also belongs to a 'clan' that has as many Buchans in it as the shore has pebbles. He once wrote that if you came from Peterhead, even if your name wasn't Buchan, it was more than likely that you had a drop of Buchan blood in you. It wasn't always like that. A list of fishermen in the Roanheads, drawn up in 1830–31, shows only one Buchan. But, according to Peter, things are now getting a bit complicated for the Buchan clan:

> For the Buchans thro' the centuries, for
>   better or for waur,
> Hae mairrit into ither tribes till gweed
>   kens fit ye are.

There are Tinkie Buchans and Royal Buchans in his poem 'The Buchan Clan', but there are no literary Buchans, not even the author's namesake, Peter Buchan, the ballad collector, who made his own distinctive mark on the North-east literary scene nearly two centuries ago. This first Peter Buchan, who was born in 1790, also wanted to go to sea, but his father was opposed to the idea. His first foray into literature came in 1814, when he published a volume of songs and verses, but he was a bad poet and the book was given a poor reception — 'a result not to be wondered at', commented William Walker, editor of *The Bards of Bon-Accord*.

So Peter went off to Edinburgh and Stirling to learn the business of printing. When he returned to Peterhead he set up the Auchmedden Press, which concentrated mainly on chapbook publishing. When sales began to flag he injected a spot of old-fashioned sex into a chapbook called *The Secret History of Macbeth*, apologising in advance for any passages that were 'rather luxuriant'.

Ugieside — 'Ugie's dear and fertile fields' — fascinated him, just as it did his namesake more than a century later. One of his poems was called 'Ravens Craig', which took its title from the same ruined castle that the present Peter Buchan discovered when he ran barefoot on Mount Pleasant as a boy. The only difference was that the Auchmedden poet saw it as a place haunted by Auld Hornie. Witches and warlocks pranced around its forbidding walls.

There were conflicting opinions on the Auchmedden poet. He was, said one critic, 'an animal with inexhaustible vanity and folly'. Others praised him for his kindness and generosity. He won his place in North-east literature through his *Gleanings of Scarce Old Ballads*. He was a friend of people like Sir Walter Scott and Charles Kirkpatrick Sharpe, and it is said that he rescued many fine ballads from oblivion. He was also the author of *Annals of Peterhead*, a slightly eccentric history of the Blue Toon, much of it composed while he was actually setting up the type on his printing press. It had little literary merit, but it was said to have 'preserved many out-of-the-way items of local history which might otherwise have been lost'.

The Peter Buchan of to-day tackles history in a different way; his prose and poetry are far removed from the ramblings of the Auchmedden printer-poet. He has been writing poetry since the 1940s. His book, 'Mount Pleasant', is a warm, sympathetic evocation of life in a north-east 'fischertoon' that has not only risen to become the principal fishing port in Europe but has also dipped its toe in North Sea oil. Like his prose works, it is full of words that have the earthy feel of Buchan about them; *sappy dubs* (wet mud), *queets* (ankles), *mishauchled* (deformed), *jobby nickles* (stinging nettles), *glaikit* and *gypit* (silly) — a rich taste of Doric that gives a salty answer to anyone who says that the old tongue is dying out. It wanders, full of wit and wisdom, through villages that were once stepping stones on the way to prosperity for Peterhead, communities that have vanished or been gobbled up by the larger centres.

It was through Peter's eyes that I saw the old Peterhead. He took me on a trip down memory lane, touching nostalgic chords at the Roanheads and the Queenie, strolling down to Buchanhaven by the Ware Road, where farmers once came with their carts to collect *ware* (seaweed) to fertilise their fields. We looked over the sea wall at Almanythie, whose natural harbour sheltered fishing boats from the Roanheads as long ago as the 18th century. The name Almanythie has given etymologists a headache, but it simply means the *auld man's hythe*, a 'hythe' (like 'hive' in Steenhive) being a harbour or a landing place.

Peter's wife, Agnes, was born in Roanheads and lived there for fifty-four years. Now a suburb, restored and renovated, it was originally the fishertown of Peterhead, a place where local fishermen settled when they were squeezed out of the port by the expansion of shipping and whaling. A Provost of Peterhead, who clearly had no vision of the future, once declared bluntly that the harbour was meant for ships, not fishing boats. There were nine boats in Roanheads in 1794, mostly operating from the harbour at Port Henry and from Almanythie. In time, as the Roanheads grew, it attracted fishermen from other small villages.

We peered up Great Stuart Street, where Peter and Agnes lived for many years. It was built in 1877 and was known as Burnie's Streetie because it was virtually taken over by fishing families from Burnhaven. The Burnies had a reputation for telling tall tales — 'binders', Peter Buchan called them, In his poem 'To a Burnie' he wrote:

> It seems to the truth ye're a stranger;
> I'm gyaun b' the binders ye tell;
> But it's a' richt wi' me,
> Tho' ye come wi' a lee,
> For I'm mair than half Burnie masel'.

Peter was 'half-Burnie' because his father was born and bred in Burnhaven. His grandfather was Andrew Buchan and the family *tee-name* was Oxy, so that Peter's father was Andrew's Oxy and Peter is Andrew's Oxy's Peter. Tee – names can be muddling to a stranger, but they are still very much in use along the north-east coast.

Burnhaven stood on the north side of Sandford Bay, across the water from Boddam. Boddam once had 151 boats and nearly 500 fishermen, but, like so many other villages, it suffered from the exodus of fishermen to Peterhead. To-day it is known for power, not podlies, for it sits in the shadow of Peterhead Power Station. Nevertheless, it is still there, which is more than can be said of its neighbour, Burnhaven.

Burnhaven has completely disappeared, wiped from the map, with nothing to show that it ever existed. Yet in 1882 there were seventy-four fishermen in the village, operating eighteen herring boats, eleven small-line boats and twenty-three yoles (small, undecked two-masted fishing boats). The decline was like a wasting disease, with the population thinning out year by year, until by 1894 only five fishermen were left in the village. By 1904–5 they were all gone.

Peter's mother came from Buchanhaven, which was then a quite independent fishertown north of Peterhead. In the middle of the 19th century it was said to be in a 'flourishing' state, with so much fish in the sea that the Buchanhaven boats came in every day laden with haddocks. But there is nothing new under the sun, for in 1864 there were complaints that the grounds were being over-fished.

When Peter's parents were married, the bride walked from Buchanhaven to Peterhead with her guests, while the 'groom walked from Burnhaven with *his* guests. The meeting place was a rope factory (now a garage) half-way between the two villages. They cleared the factory floor for the wedding celebrations and, says Peter, the feast was spoken about for a long time after. There was almost a hidden symbolism in the walk, as if the newly-weds were leaving the old ways behind and turning to Peterhead for their future. In time, the expanding port absorbed Buchanhaven, and Burnhaven became only a memory.

Peterhead takes its Blue Toon tag from the 'blue Mogganers', Moggans were stockings without feet (nowadays they are called leg-warmers and worn by fashion-conscious girls) and the 'blue Mogganers' were fishermen who wore long blue stockings. Some people believe that in chilly Peterhead the nickname had more to do with blue noses than blue stockings. Nevertheless, this cold, raw corner of Buchan has never lacked praise. As far back as the 18th century its townsfolk were said to be 'sober and courteous' and in 1795 its streets, according to the Rev. William Laing, were 'straight, clean and dry, with neatly built houses'. In 1806, Robert Forsyth said it was 'the most thriving and well-built town on the coast of Buchan'.

In the middle of the 18th century, when Peterhead was establishing a reputation as a Spa, Assembly Rooms were built on the foreshore beside the Wine Well, which was housed in a pavilion on the shore. Behind them there were a number of the 'well-built' houses mentioned by Robert Forsyth, imposing buildings with their gables to the sea. To-day, only one remains, a tall, stone house built by a sea captain in 1739. Now it is No. 5 Harbour Street, the home of Peter Buchan.

When Peter bought it eighteen years ago it was in a ruinous condition. His friends told him he was daft to even think of restoring it, but, with Agnes shaking her head in despair, he pressed on. He has two framed photographs on his wall showing what it looked like then and what it looks like now. The walls were 3 1/2 ft. thick and when he wanted to put in a bigger window in the gable he was told that if he did that the building would probably collapse. So he had the gable taken down and a new one put up.

Now the old house has regained its lost elegance. Across the street is th site of the Wine Well and the Bath House. The bath for women was said to be unrivalled in Britain, and, sitting at Peter's gable window, I thought of all the gentry and their coiffured ladies who had passed the door of No. 5 on their way to the Bath House, or walked to the famous well to sip a glass of 'sparkling nectar'. There was no wine, incidentally — 'Wine' was a corruption of the word *Wynd*. Some people sent for a bottle of water and drank it through the day; other families, living outside Peterhead, sent for a cask of water every week. The more committed health fanatics got up at five o'clock in the morning, bathed, did some exercise, and then drank the water.

The Spa, said a rapturous Dr James Beattie, provided 'converse, quiet, learning, and leisure', as well as the 'bath's enlivening tide'. But times change, and those happy images fade in the face of to-day's reality. It was expected that Peterhead would become 'the most fashionable resort in North Britain', but all that is left is an eroded carved stone in a grubby-looking car park and a spring whose water is anything but sparkling.

Over in Mount Pleasant, the old skipper muses on fish, not fashion. Round the corner from Harbour Street is Jamaica Street, where he was born and brought up. In the great days of the Spa there was a posh inn there, but when the visitors went elsewhere it deteriorated and turned into a slum. It was known in Peter's youth as the Hallelujah Lobby because the Salvation Army held services there. Now a block of council flats stands on the site.

Peter mentioned the Hallelujah Lobby in his book, *Fisher Blue*, recalling an old lady there who sold tin kettles and was called 'Pots and Pans'. 'The old dear was rather fond of gin,' he said, 'and in those days when it was quite permissible for a boddie's doorstep to project half across the pavement, she was very often in a horizontal position, with her birn of tin-ware rattling aboot her lugs.'

From the window of Mount Pleasant, the dark scar of the Skerry Rock can be seen jutting up from the sea off Boddam Harbour. Peter told me of the day his father, who was just a 'loon' then, was in a 'ripper-boatie' near the Skerry with two companions when a whaler passed, homeward bound for Dundee. Someone on board hailed them, asking if they would take a message ashore. A note from the captain was passed down, with instructions to go to the post office in Peterhead and send a telegram to Dundee saying the ship would be home next morning. There was a shilling enclosed to cover the cost, and they were told they could keep the change. Peter's father was the only one in the boat who could read, so he got the job — and ended up with a sixpence in his pocket. 'It wis a lang time afore he saw anither een,' said Peter.

We sat at his window and looked across the harbour to the land of the Queenie Arabs. The two islands of Keith Inch and Greenhill were at one time separated by a channel called the Poolmouth and linked to the mainland by a causeway known as the Queenie, or Quinzie, which was covered at high tide. People spoke about going 'ower the Queenie'. Now they talk about living on the Queenie, but if they are doing that, says Peter, they are living on water. The fact is that the name has come to apply to the area covered by Keith Inch and Greenhill, which is now reached by a bridge.

There are oils tanks and industrial buildings on the Queenie, but blocked-up windows in one of the warehouses are a reminder that people once lived there, 'on top of each other,' according to Peter. He remembers going into one of these houses on a Hogmanay with a jar of syrup for his 'first-foot.' People who were born and brought up on Keith Inch were known as Queenie Arabs. It wasn't a derogatory term, but it set them apart from the townsfolk across the water. Walk around the harbour and you'll find a boat called the *Queenie Arab*; in fact, Peter couldn't remember the time when there wasn't a boat in Peterhead with the name Queenie Arab. In his poem, 'Div Ye Mind', he described how he and his pals met in a 'stave-built hoosie wi' a can'le in a tin':

An' there the bigger loons amon's
Wid mak' a wily plan
To fecht the Queenie Arabs
Or some ither war-like clan.

Peter went back to school in later life — as a teacher. When he gave up fishing and came ashore he got a job for a year as an uncertificated teacher at Crimond School. His subjects were maths and geography and he made it clear from the first day, *before* he started teaching, that if anyone tried to play him up he would be in trouble. He never had any trouble.

On one occasion, when asked about long division, he said he would show them on the board how it was done. He began to work it out with chalk and the sum got longer and longer. As he pulled down the board to get extra space for his scribbles he realised that there was something wrong. Finally, one boy said, 'Please, sir, you've made a mistake.' Peter called him out and told him to show where the mistake was. The boy pointed to part of the sum. 'There,' he said.

'Well,' said Peter, 'you're the only one in the class to notice my deliberate mistake, so you're excused homework for the rest of the week.' After that, he had to put in deliberate mistakes because the pupils looked for them — so that they wouldn't have to do homework.

Peter was in alien territory at Crimond — a *fisher* teaching farming folk! He was sometimes reminded of it in a less than friendly way. When he remarked in front of his colleagues that he had learned some new words at Crimond, words that Buchan farming folk used, one woman teacher sneered, 'Better than fisher, anyway.' The gulf between farming and fishing has always been there; it was why many communities had, and still have, their separate Seatowns. A Cullen minister said a century ago that fishers were 'a distinct class of society, with sentiments, sympathies and habits peculiar to themselves', and it is still true today. The north-east writer, John R. Allan, commenting on the great difference between fishermen and country folk, said, perhaps with his tongue in his cheek, that we should think of fishers as people who of necessity make their homes on shore, but so mistrust the land that they build on the very edge of the waves and shun intercourse with the land dwellers.

Peter Buchan, who himself lives on the edge of the sea, would have no truck with such a sentiment, although he believes there is still a big gulf between farmers and fishers. A few years ago, when he was editor of the Buchan Heritage Society's magazine, *Heirskip*, he wrote, 'For all that they know of each other, they could be on separate planets.' As president of the Heritage Society, he did his best to close the gap. After his teaching year at Crimond, he travelled around the north-east for the Caledonian Oil Company and learned more about farming folk than he had done in all his days as a fisher.

Yet, despite his flirtation with the land, the fisher poet of Peterhead has come back to the sea. He ended his working life as traffic controller at Peterhead Harbour, watching over the endless coming and going of the boats that crowd this bustling Buchan port. The Blue Toon has seen great fishing prosperity in recent years, but on the first-floor landing of Peter's house there is a photograph that puts it in perspective. It was taken about 1929, in those heady days when everyone in Buchan seemed to be heading south for the herring fishing.

The picture shows a long line of fishing boats, two and three abreast, sailing into Yarmouth, a fisher fleet that tailed back in a great curve until it disappeared from sight. At a rough count there are forty boats in the picture — and that, I learned later, was about one-twentieth of the fleet. In the lead as they enter the harbour are three vessels — a Zulu, a Fifie called the *White Heather* (both motorised), and the Peterhead steam drifter *Twinkling Star*, with Peter's father at the wheel. It was his boat — he was the skipper. The photograph was taken in the days when you could see 1,000 boats at Yarmouth.

Upstairs, on another landing, there is a coloured photograph of a more modern fishing boat, also called the *Twinkling Star*. It was Peter's boat, which he skippered for twelve years. His thoughts on being a skipper were summed up in his poem, 'Stormy Bank':

It's fine to hae the skipper's job
If luck signs on as mate,
For then ye're ca'd an eident, clivver chiel,
But should that mate desert ye, weel,
The job's nae jist so great,
For then ye're ca'd an eident, eeseless feel.

When Peter retired he bought a boat, *Sweet Promise*. It is more than likely that he planned to catch a few ripper codlings.

The ripper mannie's a hardy breed!
There's naething but codlins in his heid.

The ripper is 'a primitive yet effective way of catching cod without bait', but some people have a different way of describing it. 'A lump o' lead at ae end an' a feel at the ither', is one of them. So far, Peter's new boat hasn't lived up to its promise, mostly because Peter has had problems with his health. When he was in hospital last year I went to visit him and discovered that he was regarded as a celebrity. Everybody knew that he was in 'dock' for an overhaul. 'Fit like, Skipper?' asked a complete stranger.

The only thing missing from No. 5 Mount Pleasant is the sight of 'five-an-twenty ripper codlins dryin' at the door', otherwise the Skipper is content. 'Dive ye mind?' is the title of one of his poems. What *he* remembers is that barefoot boy on Mount Pleasant ... the time when 'the loons gid dookin'' with 'nae a stitch o' claes'... the bonny summer days when 'the tar cam' up atween oor taes'... the jaunts to the curing yards when they splashed through 'lochs o' pickle bree an' seas o' sappy dubs'.

As for the future, that can take care of itself. 'We dinna ken fit lies ahead,' he says, 'So let's look back — an' lauch.'

CHAPTER SIX
Farewell tae Tarwathie

The farm of Tarwathie is just over two miles north of Strichen, almost in the lap of Mormond Hill. It was in this corner of Buchan more than a century ago that a young farm lad turned his back on the land and went off to the Greenland whaling to make his fortune. Whether or not he was successful nobody knows; no one can remember his name, or what happened to him. But he gave Tarwathie its fleeting moment of glory in a song that was sung on the ships that sailed to the northern seas.

Farewell tae Tarwathie, adieu Mormond Hill,
And the dear land o' Crimond I bid ye farewell,
I'm bound out for Greenland and ready to sail
In hopes to find riches in hunting the whale.

There are three Tarwathies at the foot of Mormond — West, South and North. The folk there have all tried to find out the name of the lad in that old whaling song. Several people told me they had heard it sung on Robbie Shepherd's radio programme, and Sandy Lowe, who was out on the moss cutting peat when I spoke to him, sent me down to South Tarwathie to talk to his wife, Marlene. She had a long-playing record called 'Whales and Nightingales,' sung by Judy Collins, and on it you could hear the crying of the whales.

Marlene dug out the LP and dusted it off, and it scraped into life. Sitting in that Buchan farm kitchen, we were suddenly pitched into the icy wastes of Greenland. Behind the voice of the singer could be heard the wailing of the whales, a sad sound, as if they were crying out against the fate that had overtaken them in the shape of hunters with murderous harpoons and blubber knives in their hands.

'You wouldn't play it to cheer yourself up,' said Marlene.

Later, I discovered that *Farewell tae Tarwathie* was in a collection of whaling songs brought together by Gavin Greig, the Buchan folk-song collector, and that it was written in the middle of last century by George Scroggie, a miller at Fedderate, New Deer. Greig was anxious to get more whaling songs for his collection, along with information about them, for he was concerned that 'the local whaling minstrelsy' would die out when the Greenland men had gone.

His fears were well-founded, for, although popular songs like *Farewell tae Tarwathie* and *The Diamond Ship* have been preserved, many have been lost, particularly the crude choruses sung by the Greenland men as they toiled at the capstan before leaving port. Gavin Greig thought that some of the words were 'rather strong for print,' and John Cranna, the Fraserburgh historian, said that the choruses were 'sometimes so lewd as not to bear recalling.'

The identity of the lad from Tarwathie remains a mystery. Dr David Bertie, deputy curator of the Arbuthnott Museum in Peterhead, said that very often these old songs went the rounds, the names and places being changed to suit different areas. He thought it possible that this might have happened to the Tarwathie song and, in fact, there are different versions of it. The one sung by Judy Collins has five stanzas, while another version has an extra verse wishing luck to 'the bonnie ship.'

'The king of that country is the fierce Greenland bear,' runs a line of the song. Inside the Arbuthnott Museum you can see the 'King' himself — a huge, stuffed Polar bear. The museum staff called it Snowy, but it hasn't exactly got a Persil-white look, even though it had been given a wash shortly before my visit. The whalemen often came home with bears they had shot, but this one is said to have been brought back alive. It is supposed to have got off the ship, lumbered through the town, and walked into a pub. Not surprisingly, Dr Bertie takes that story with a pinch of salt. Snowy must have been dead, he says, but he has never been able to find out when it arrived in Peterhead or when it was presented to the museum.

The museum has an interesting display of whaling relics, including harpoons, samples of whale oil, and a knife used by the 'blubber-hunters.' The liquid in those sample bottles gave the North-east it's first oil boom. Whale oil was used for street lamps – 'best boiled whale oil for the public lamps of this city,' read an advertisement in an Aberdeen newspaper in 1830 – and it was in demand as an industrial lubricant, for soap-making, dressing wool and vegetable fibres, and for currying leather. Whale oil, wrote William Thom in 1811, was 'an indispensable necessity of life,' and whale fishing was 'of the highest national importance.'

The year 1851 marked a high point in the hunt for whales. Aberdeen, Peterhead, Fraserburgh, Banff and Montrose all sent ships to the Arctic. Peterhead had thirty-two ships sailing to Greenland in 1857, compared with Aberdeen, which had fourteen vessels whaling out of the port in the 1820s. Banff, which suffered a heavy financial loss when a ship was wrecked in 1820, tried abain in the 1850s, but finally abandoned whaling in 1856. Fraserburgh, which sent a single ship to the northern waters in 1852, had expanded to six whalers by 1858. Most of them were bought from other ports, two of them from Banff and Peterhead in 1855.

The only whales the North-east is likely to encounter nowadays are the small marine mammals which can sometimes be seen close inshore. When I was in the Mearns, I heard about a dead whale that had been washed up in the salmon nets at Skateraw, Newtonhill, in 1913. The fishermen cut it up and buried it to get rid of the smell. Someone wrote a verse about it —

Here lies a whale of Scripture fame,
Which carried Jonah o'er the main,
He'll roam no more, make no man wrench,
He's buried deep to hide the stench.

Later, when I was talking to Peter Buchan about whales, and in particular about whales being seen near the shore, he said that they came in after the herring. 'They're like a fish meal factory,' he remarked. 'Get on the wrong side of a whale when it blows and the smell is appalling.' Lots of people thought that the Biblical story of Jonah and the Whale was untrue, but he wasn't one of them. 'A whale could swallow a horse,' he said. He recalled hearing about a Faroese or Icelandic fisherman who was swallowed by a whale and later found alive inside its belly.

When the fortune-seeking farm worker from Tarwathie left for the Greenland waters, he would have been able to see his beloved Mormond as his ship sailed north from one of the Buchan ports. The words of an old couplet would have been in his mind as they passed Rattray Head

Keep Mormond Hill a handspike high
And Rattray Briggs ye'll ne'er come nigh.

Behind Rattray Head was a fishing village with a name that had a chilly ring about it. The Arctic whalers had to endure the harsh conditions of Baffin Bay; Buchan fishers had to suffer the rigours of Botany Bay. The real name of the village was Seatown of Rattray, but when it was established in 1795 criminals were being shipped from Aberdeen to Botany Bay in Australia and the fishers who settled in this cold, windy corner of Buchan quickly adopted 'Botany' as the name of their own settlement.

Life was hard at Botany. In the late 1830s, six or seven families abandoned this treacherous stretch of coast and went to live in Burnhaven — the Burnies — and by 1841 there were no fishers left in Botany. An attempt was made a number of years later to revive fishing at Rattray, but it met with only partial success. In the first half of this century the last families at Botany died off and the houses were allowed to fall into ruin.

The whalers siphoned off many fishermen from villages like Botany. There was a time when a string of these fishtowns lay along the coast between Fraserburgh and Peterhead, tiny communities that lived on a knife-edge of poverty, their inhabitants moving from one settlement to the other in an attempt to improve their lot. They were drawn to new fishtowns like Rattray by promises of 'fine cod,' improved landing places, and the local laird's assurance that 'every convenience will be attended to.' To-day, many of them have vanished, with nothing to show that they ever existed.

The old fishing settlements stood on a coastline feared by mariners. The infamous Rattray Briggs claimed their share of stricken ships, among them the s.s. *Union*, which ran aground in 1870, with over 400 passengers and crew on board. No lives were lost, but police from as far away as Aberdeen were called in to deal with looters. In 1874, the *Grace Darling* battled against a gale, struggled past Rattray, and was driven ashore near the present outlet of the Loch of Strathbeg. The sole survivor was found barely alive on the beach at Corskelly the following morning.

Corskelly, which stood just south of the present village of St Combs, was one of the 'lost' fishertowns. Some people think there was another vanished village called Boatlea beside it, but a few years ago, in his book *Fishing off the Knuckle*, David W. Summers, who was born at Charlestown, argued that Corskelly and Boatlea were one of the same place. He said that the official name of the village was Seatown of Corskelly, while Boatlea was 'the name most probably used by the inhabitants themselves.'

So were there two 'lost' villages or one? To an outsider the arguments are confusing, but Andrew Forsyth, the Corskelly blacksmith, took me behind his 'smiddy' and pointed to an overgrown track running east through two fields. A rounded pillar stuck up from one of the fields. There were originally two pillars, and two more farther on, and they marked a track, still a right-of-way, that led to the Seatown of Corskelly. So where was Boatlea? Andy pointed to some cottages to the left. 'There,' he said.

At one time the old track ran down to the sea. I followed it until it took me on to a road leading to Corskelly Cottages, where I met Dugald Innes, Andrew Forsyth's nephew. He said that when they were ploughing the field behind us — on Corskelly Farm — he had seen what seemed to be the remains of a number of middens, with signs of ash. There had also been a lot of mussels in the field — and mussels were used as bait by the fishermen.

He sent me down the road to another group of cottages — Boatlea Cottages – where I met an elderly couple, Jessie Duncan and her brother Joe. I asked them where the village of Boatlea had been. 'Here,' said Jessie, slapping the table. 'You're in it!' Joe and Jessie said that Boatlea had been a small hamlet, with about five or six cottages. Three remained, and they had seen the 'founds' of two others nearby. They told me that the spot where Corsekelly had been was down by the old track I had taken, past the pillars, in a field on Corsekelly Farm known as the Pasture Park.

Joe, who has been at Corsekelly for forty years and was formerly grieve on the farm, said that when the Pasture Park was 'broken up' (ploughed over) they came upon the 'founds' of between fourteen and twenty houses. Jessie had heard that a lot of the people in Corsekelly had been skippers. She also thought that Boatlea was in existence before Corsekelly. If they were correct, there were two villages, but, like the Siamese twin towns of Inverallochy and Cairnbulg, and Charlestown and St Combs, they had been so close to each other that they had been almost like one. I left it at that; the experts could argue over it, I thought, but it seemed to me that it was anybody's guess.

There were eleven fisher families at Corsekelly at the end of the 17th century. In 1730 there were five boats and two yoles in the village, with six boats and one yole operating the following year. The death knell for the village was sounded in 1785 when St Combs was established. Twenty families had moved to the new village by 1795. St Combs and Corsekelly were on different estates, but in the late 18th century both came under one owner and the old Seatown of Corsekelly was phased out in favour of St Combs.

Long before Corsekelly was finally abandoned, a number of families had migrated to another new village — Drumlinie. It stood near the old church of St Fergus, and its official name was Seatown of St Fergus. Peter Buchan, the ballad collector, called it Drum Lithe. His mother belonged to Drumlinie and, in fact, most of the villagers — seven of them in 1770 — were Buchans from Boatlea. The last man to live in Drumlinie was a Buchan — Alexander Buchan. That was in 1800.

Nearly two centuries later, all traces of the village have gone, lost in the barren links that stretch away to Rattray and the Broch. There was a familiar reason for its short life. Looking back on the attempt to establish a fishtown at Drumlinie, the *Statistical Account* said in the later 18th century: 'If there were a proper landing place for the boats,it would be an excellent station for fishers, being so near to Rattrayhead which has long been esteemed the very best fishing ground for cod and ling.' The fact is that there is no suitable landing place — and Drumlinie died.

Bleak though it is to-day, with only the ugly bulk of the St Fergus gas terminal to break the monotony, in Peter Buchan's time this part of the coast boasted 'one of the most extensive and pleasant downs in Scotland, extending several miles along the coast.' Parts of it were cultivated and it was, according to Buchan, 'often frequented by those who took pleasure in the healthy exercise of the golf and horse-riding.' Even then, however, it may have been declining in popularity, for Buchan added, 'Such salubrious sports are now seldom practised.'

Nowadays, one of the less salubrious sports is practised by youngsters racing up and down the road to the old kirkyard on motor tricycles, throwing up dust and damaging the dunes; by poachers looking for a pheasant or two; and by people walking their dogs on the links in the belief that it is public property. The road to the kirkyard is a right-of-way, but the land around it is owned by John Chalmers, who was sitting on his tractor outside his farm at North Kirton when I met him. 'I've lived here every day of my life,' he said. 'It's a quiet place.' He wants to keep it that way.

John has never come across anything that looks like the remains of Drumlinie, although some people claim they have found some ruins. It is a remote and desolate corner of coastal Buchan, and even the ebullient Peter Buchan seemed to be driven into a state of gloom by the auld kirkyard — 'the place of skulls,' he called it. It was, he said, a place for anyone who wanted to get some 'mournful pleasure' from contemplating those who were 'mouldering into dust' at their feet. Taking his advice and giving a passing thought to 'the transitory state of men,' I left the ancient tombstones and headed for Sodom.

I have never been able to find out why Charlestown came to be known as Sodom. One helpful Sodomite told me it had something to do with a porter and ale establishment that existed there. The St Combs people are blamed for giving Charlestown its bad name — and they still call it Sodom, according to the locals. There has always been rivalry between the two communities. St Combs was laid out in 1784, and the folk in the 'New Toon' took a poor view when Charlestown was established six years later, hence the 'Sodom' taunt. The two villages are so close together that you can't tell where one ends and the other begins, except that there are road signs indicating the whereabouts of Charlestown. This may have been a token gesture to Charlestown folk who didn't like the idea of their village being swallowed up by St Combs.

Sodom isn't the only village to land up with a peculiar nickname. The St Combs inhabitants themselves have one — *Kwities*. Nobody is very sure how that one came about. One rather puzzling theory is that it had something to do with guillemots, which are also called 'kwites.' Along the coast, the natives of Cairnbulg are known as 'Bulgers.' In the old days, the fishermen wore sky-blue jackets, which folk in Fraserburgh called 'the Bulger's vomit.' Not everyone said Bulger; some said Bilger. William M. Alexander, in his *Place-Names of Aberdeenshire*, said that Cyarnbulg was how the landward people pronounced it, while fishermen pronounced it Cyarnbilg.

Even then, there are still ends to tie up in this confusing name game. For instance, the Seatown of Inverallochy was once known as 'Cotton' because hemp was grown there, and the residents are still called Cottoners. There is, however, another theory that the name 'Cotton' had its origin in a cot-town that at one time existed near the village. On top of all that, there was also a name used by the St Combs fishermen to describe the joint villages of Inverallochy and Cairnbulg. They called it Wheelick.

There are a number of twin towns facing each other in eyeball to eyeball confrontation along the North-east coast, and it is a fair bet that rivalry still exists in many of them, although it may be more muted nowadays. St Combs and Charlestown, which are separated by a burn, have hurled insults across that strip of water for as long as people can remember. Sixty years ago, the writer Peter Anson said there was 'a strong clannish feeling between the natives of the respective sides of this stream, which in old days almost amounted to an antagonism.' Round about the same time, the *Aberdeen Press and Journal* described Inverallochy and Cairnbulg as 'two enemy camps regarding each other from afar, each keeping well to his own side of the burn.'

The sign at the entrance to the two villages says 'Cairnbulg and Inverallochy,' but farther on the road forks and two signs indicate Cairnbulg to the left and Inverallochy to the right. Go through Cairnbulg and you come out on a rough, stony road that passes the coastguard station and ends up at the harbour. There was only a single pier here until a few years ago, but now another wall has turned it into a neat little harbour.

Peter Anson, in his *Fishing Boats and Fishing Folk*, mentioned the earlier pier, which turned out to be almost useless. At that time, in the late 1920s, the fishing fleet of the two villages totalled sixty-seven boats, including thirteen steam drifters. 'Within the last quarter of a century,' wrote Anson, 'there has been a steady decrease in the population, among which there are no more than 125 fishermen — more than three hundred less than sixty years ago.'

When I made my way down to Inverallochy, I found a solitary boat lying on the foreshore. It reminded me of Peter Anson's description of what happened in the past. All the larger fishing craft belonging to Cairnbulg and Inverallochy had to lie up at Fraserburgh between seasons, and the remainder were hauled on to the beach. It was a hard, risky business, for, as Anson said, 'no more exposed and wind-swept beach can be imagined.' Most of the boats were drawn right up between the houses or placed on to the low, rocky shore. They lay attached to posts, just above high-water mark.

Round the corner in Shore Street I found a link with the old fishing days — Maggie's Hoosie. This red-roofed, rubble-built cottage at No. 26 Shore Street is believed to have been built about the middle of the 18th century. Gordon District Council have plans to restore it as a museum of life in 19th century fishing villages, but some local people are sceptical about the plan.

'Naebody will come here tae see that,' said one, 'and even if anybody did it widna be Maggie's Hoosie.' Maggie was Maggie Duthie, a spinster who lived on her own. Her house had a sand floor and old-fashioned crockery on the shelves, but everything inside it was removed. It stood empty for forty years, but about two years ago the council put a new roof on the building and boarded up the windows.

I couldn't help thinking that Maggie would probably have been happy to think that life had come back to her 'hoosie' on the edge of the sea.

CHAPTER SEVEN
Sails and Sea-dogs

The grey emptiness of the sea spread as far as the eye could see. Looking north from Kinnaird Head lighthouse, I thought of the whalers that had come out of that vast expanse of water on their way home from Greenland, carrying a fortune in blubber and bone in their holds. Their first landmark was Kinnaird Head — 'the outermost edge of Buchan.' If they came at night, the bright eye of the lighthouse beckoned them towards the Buchan coast. There were no revolving lights in those early days. Instead, an array of fixed lamps were backed up by a series of parabolic reflectors — seventeen in all, lined up like soldiers on parade. In clear weather, they could be seen fourteen miles off the coast, and the power that drove them was whale oil.

The Greenland men boasted that they would come back 'wi' a ship full o' oil,' but another kind of oil came from thé sea, not from whales, but from sea dogs. Sea dogs were dogfish, small sharks, whose livers were much in demand for the oil they produced. The carcases were used as manure. No less than 70,000 sea dogs were scattered over the Mains of Crimonmogate, west of the Loch of Strathbeg, in the first decade of the 19th century, no doubt casting an unimaginable stench over the Buchan countryside.

The catching of seadogs was common in many of the smaller fish towns around the coast. In the late 18th century, reporting on the different types of seasonal fishing, the *Statistical Account for Kincardine* said that one form of fishing was 'the dog line.' 'In August the sea dog, that voracious fish, consuming all before it, comes to 4 and 3 leagues (about ten miles) from shore, sometimes nearer, and is taken in considerable quantities, 20 yielding, when good, one Scotch pint of oil from the liver.'

During the 19th century, seadogs infested the fishing grounds in the way that locusts were a plague on the land, causing serious damage to the herring fishing. The worst 'dogfish' years were the 1860s. These razor-toothed marauders attacked the herring nets when they were full of fish, ripped them apart, cleaned them of herring, and left them severely damaged. There were times when the sea was alive with dogfish.

The herring catches were so badly affected that in 1850 the Fishery Board asked the Fraserburgh fishery officer to examine the feasibility of abandoning herring fishing for dogfishing, which they thought might be more profitable. The fishery officer's report recalled that forty or fifty years earlier the fishermen in Fraserburgh had gone in for dogfishing and pointed out that the price for oil then was much higher. He thought it unlikely that the fishermen would go back to dogfishing.

The year 1865 saw the dogfish war reach its climax. The damage done was worse than ever before, but it was also the last year of the seadog raids. From then on their numbers diminished until they virtually disappeared. The herring catches began to increase and the boats went farther afield in their search for fish. Despite a cholera outbreak in 1866, the catch for that season reached an impressive total of 400,221 crans.

They came in their hundreds for the East Coast herring fishing, by train from Inverness, Sutherland, Ross and the Western Isles — fishers, crofters, tramps, dealers and preachers. Whole families arrived on the boats taking part in the fishing, carrying their beds, blankets and household goods on the vessels. A Fraserburgh poet said that along the coast 'five thousand boats will whiles appear.' The Broch had its share of them —

Six hundred herrin' boats or more
In July range about that shore.

When they left for the fishing grounds, the horizon was blotted out by their brown sails, and when they came back at the end of August, lying within a mile or two of the shore as they shot their nets in the gloaming, they hoisted their lights. Light after light pierced the darkness, spreading for miles across the water, so that watchers on the shore could see what appeared to be a brightly-lit city on the sea. People turned out to catch a glimpse of this fairy-land.

The lights have long gone out on Fraserburgh's great herring boom — that 'piscatory Klondyke,' as one writer called it. To-day, Peterhead is the premier fishing port, but the Broch is unlikely to be troubled by the Blue Toon's prosperity, for the old rivalry between the two ports seems to be disappearing. Faithlie was the original name of the burgh, and, like Tam in a well-known J. C. Milne poem, Fraserburgh folk still say, 'Gie me auld Faithlie toon,' although nowadays they say it less abrasively.

On the other hand, both towns keep a canny eye on each other, just as they did in the past. A pile of visitors' books in Kinnaird Head lighthouse, which overlooks Faithlie harbour, has signatures going back to the end of last century. The first book is dated 1894 and the first signature is that of James Innes, assistant keeper at the lighthouse, who could scarcely be described as a visitor. The first *real* visitor was Alex Wiseman, from Fraserburgh, and after that they poured in, sometimes as many as thirty a day. On June 25, 1894, a large party from Peterhead arrived — they had come to see what the Brochers were up to with their grand lighthouse.

Peterhead visitors are likely to be in front of the queue again, for the lighthouse, which this year became automatic, is to be Scotland's first lighthouse museum. Visitors who climb to the lighthouse platform will find themselves standing on two layers of Scottish history, for Kinnaird Head is not only Scotland's oldest lighthouse, it was built on top of a castle that reaches back two more centuries to 1570. The buildings at its feet, which will house the museum exhibits, were built in 1830.

Jim Oliver, the principal keeper at Kinnaird Head until it became automatic, has served on a number of stations, including remote ones like Cape Wrath and the Pentland Skerries. The Penland station was rough. 'The tide moved so fast that when you looked down you thought it was the lighthouse that was moving,' he said. Standing with him on the platform, we were looking down at something less turbulent, for on the foreshore was another piece of Broch history. This was the Wine Tower, a curious block-like structure used at one time as a chapel.

They say that a piper who fell in love with the laird's daughter was locked up in a cave beneath the tower. He drowned when the tide came in and his grief-stricken lover killed herself by leaping from the top of the tower on to the rocks. Some people claim that the piper's ghost can be heard playing for his lost love, but it is more likely to be the sound of seals, for the cave is known as the Selch's Hole. The word 'selchs' means seals and there were, and probably still are, large colonies of them on the Buchan coast. Lady Anne Drummond, Countess of Erroll, said that one of the most remarkable things in the district was 'the multitude of selches that come in at Strathbegge.'

The panoramic view from the top of the lighthouse is breath-taking. On a clear day you can see the peaks of Sutherland. Officially, the Kinnaird light could be spotted from a distance of 25 miles, but one old skipper who sailed on coasters off the Buchan coast said he had seen the loom of it at 40 miles. The loom or glow is what you see when the flash goes up; you don't actually see the flash.

One by one, we picked off the landmarks ... the towering chimney stack of Boddam power station ... Mormond Hill and its masts ... little Rosehearty snoozing in the sun ... Cairnbulg Point ... the massive snout of Troup Head, said to be one of of the finest viewpoints in Scotland. Not far from the shore a mackerel boat sat idly on the water. Below us, a lobster boat came chugging into the harbour.

It was calm and peaceful, but it isn't always like that, and Jim Oliver had a register of wrecks to prove it. The first entry in the book was a report on the *ss St Clement*, a schooner from Aberdeen, which was wrecked on the Cairnbulg Briggs, three miles from the lighthouse. The captain was not on board at the time and the reason for the loss of the vessel, which was valued at £6000, was given as 'Want of judgement on the part of the man in charge in coming too near the land.' The ship was carrying a cargo of fresh fish.

Seven miles west of Fraserburgh are the ruins of Dundarg Castle, an untidy rickle of stones set on a narrow, red sandstone promontory high above the tempermental tides of Aberdour

Bay. It is all that is left of a medieval castle that was built on the site of a great Iron Age fort, Dun Dearg, the Red Fort, which dated from A.D. 300. Below, the waves wash over the wide, flat rocks where the ill-fated *Edward Bonaventure* broke up when she was driven ashore in a storm in 1556.

The ship carried important people and a valuable cargo and Dorothy Dunnett, a meticulous researcher, gave some idea of what was in the cargo when she wrote about the wrecking of the *Bonaventure* in her novel, *The Ringed Castle*.

> The *Edward Bonaventure*, with her cargo. With her six timbers of sables, from the Emperor to the monarchs of England. Twenty entire sables, exceedingly beautiful, with teeth, ears and claws. With four once-living sables, with chains and with collars. With thirty lynx furs, large and beautiful, and six great skins, very rich and rare, worn only by the Emperor for worthiness. And a large and fair white jerfalcon, upon which the wild swan, crane, geese and other fowls might look down on as she floated dead on the Bay of Pitsligo.

Dorothy Dunnett said that some of the cargo was transferred 'swiftly and effectively into the pockets of Buchan,' but some people believe that valuables from the Bonaventure were hidden around the Red Fort and that they are still there, waiting, perhaps, for some 20th century treasure hunter.

Another Scottish novelist, Catherine Gavin, whose relatives came from Sauchentree, used Quarry Head, less than a mile from Dundarg Castle, as the setting for her first novel, *The Hostile Shore*. 'A stranger walking on the cliffs,' she wrote, 'might never have suspected the existence of a village below unless, venturing near the edge, he had seen smoke rising from the chimneys, or gone out upon the grassy promontory of Quarry Head to look down upon the bay, with the cottages, set end-on to the sea, clustering about the little harbour.'

The rough road down to the shore, which 'fell away from the modern world' to wind between cliffs pink with sea daisies, is still much the same as described in the book. Catherine Gavin said it had seen little change 'since Charlie's men scattered after Culloden and Lord Pitsligo threw himself upon the mercy of his fisherfolk of Dundargue.' In the winter of 1746–7, Alexander Fraser, the fourth and last Lord Pitsligo, hid from the Hanoverians, in a cave near Quarry Head, but it is now blocked up. There is, in fact, no village of Dundargue; there never was — its thirty granite houses, with their gables to the sea, existed only in Catherine Gavin's imagination.

There is a piece of old weather lore about Aberdour which local folk say is usually correct —

Fin the rumble comes fae Pittendrum
The ill weather's a' tae cum,
Fin the rumble comes fae Aberdour
The ill weather's a' ower.

Pittendrum is near Sandhaven and the rumble is the noise of the waves on the pebbly shore. Where it was rumbling on 27th October, 1884, is anybody's guess, but the ill weather that descended on Aberdour Bay that night almost cost fifteen men their lives — and brought fame to Aberdour's own 'Grace Darling.'

Down in the bay, on the site of an old woollen mill, a farm worker called James Whyte lived with his wife, Jane, and their five boys and four girls. On that fateful night in 1884, when gales were battering the Buchan coast, the Dundee steamer *William Hope* drifted helplessly off Aberdour after its engine had failed near Troup Head. It was driven on to the rocks in Aberdour Bay and Jane Whyte, who had gone to check on her husband's small boat, found the steamer lying a short distance from the shore, half submerged in the raging sea. She plunged into the water to catch a rope thrown by one of the men, wound it round her body, and struggled back to the shore. One by one, the fifteen members of the crew hauled themselves to safety using the rope held by Jane. She was awarded an RNLI silver medal for her bravery and to-day a memorial on the site of her cottar home commemorates the event.

This is a fascinating stretch of coast, dotted with farms that have intriguing names like Poukburn, and Ironhill, or Eernel; Merryhillock and Happyhillock, whose names appear to mean just what they say, and Egypt, which has nothing to do with camels, although there is a sign showing a camel at the end of the farm road. The name is thought to have its origin in the Egyptians, or gypsies, who wandered about this corner of Buchan at one time. Even the rocks and caves have tantalising names. Lord Pitsligo's Cave was originally known as the Cave of Cowshaven, and there is also a Reid Coo's Haven. Near the Cowshaven cave is the Cat's Hole, or Cat's Eye, which had an entrance from the sea and another from the top of the cliff, but the local council filled it up with rubbish.

A local writer, Mrs Mary Michie, who wrote a tourist guide to the Aberdour shore, told me of some more ... Maw's Craig (a maw is a seagull, and the rock is usually covered with gulls), the Oily Pig, which is black and shaped like a pig, the Hasses, which probably means a gap or an opening, and the Barn Door, which looks just like a barn door. She found an interesting one in an old map of 1871 — the Slack of the Red Shinn — but was never able to find out what it meant. A slack is a pass, and a 'shinn' is the slope of a hill, so here again it probably had a topographical meaning.

The ruined church and kirkyard of St Drostan's stands above the Dour Burn, beside the main road to the bay. There is an unusual 19th century doocot near the gate, which, incidentally, was gifted by Catherine Gavin. The old kirkyard is full of interesting tombstones, but one that caught my eye was over the grave of a local man who must have been known as the Happy Bachelor. His name was Peter Walker. He worked at the local mill and died in 1869, and the inscription on his stone says that he 'lived in single blessedness for nearly 70 years, a pattern of contentment.' There could be no more persuasive argument for bachelordom than that.

Not far from the kirk, a rough road runs west past the farms of Bankhead and Clinterty. This was the old mail coach road from Aberdour to Pennan. Mary Michie, who is now in her eighties, lives at Bankhead. Behind her house, she looks across the fields to the great sweep of the bay and the cliffs of Dundarg, where the *Edward Bonaventure* went to its doom. Mary had heard that the locals helped themselves to the ship's goods. West of Bankhead, the fields roll away to Darder Hill, which is the boundary line of the 400 acre farm. To the north, the farmland drops towards the cliffs, where a waterfall tumbles down to the shore beside the Darder Rock.

This sheltered corner is known as the Cyard's Cove, taking its name from cyards or tinkers who once lived there. Here, there is a huge rock called the Auld Wife's Loup, where one of the tinker women committed suicide. Just round the corner from the cove is an arch called Pitjossie, although it is better known to local folk as the Needle's Eye.

This part of the Buchan coast is riddled with caves, many of them used at one time or another as makeshift homes. Not all the 'residents' were tinkers. The best-known cave in the Aberdour area is the Hermit's Cave, below the Darder Rock, and the hermit was a retired sea captain, David Reid. It can be reached by the shore when the tide is out. Although low and cramped for space, there was enough room in it for the Captain's bed and a few of his possessions.

The stream from the waterfall provided the Captain with a steady supply of water, and he grew his own vegetables in a patch of ground beside it. Mary Michie remembers seeing his 'cabbage patch' when she went to Aberdour beach with a school picnic as a child. She never saw the Hermit, but she saw his blue and black valor stove outside his door.

That was in the 1920s. She recently wrote a story about the Hermit, part fact, part fiction, and it is an intriguing tale. Alex Laird, who was the Bankead farmer at the time, came upon the Captain trying to light a fire outside the cave. Few people knew his real name; to most people he was just 'Jock,' and the cave came to be known as Jock's Cave. The Captain built up the entrance to it and fitted up an old door which he found in an out-house on the farm. He made two containers from fish boxes, one to hold his clothes, the other for his pots and crockery. They doubled up as a table and seat. His bed was a heather-covered ledge in the rocks, his pillow a sack stuffed with chaff.

'On a bonny summer's day, with the murmur of waves as they gently lapped the shore, the cave would have been a haven of tranquility and contentment,' said Mary Michie, in her notes on the Hermit of Aberdour, 'but in the long dark winter days and stormy seas lashing the rocks in spume it would have been a place of desolation, so wet and cold, yet he stopped on.' He was offered a bed in the farm 'chaumer,' but he declined it. He never sought shelter from his neighbours.

He was friendly with the Aberdour folk, but also secretive, never speaking of his past. He got milk and eggs from the women on the farm, and sometimes bannocks and scones, and in return he carried pails of peat or water for them, or fired their boiler, or mucked out the henhouse. He also made heather pot scrubbers and 'besoms' (brushes), and he collected gulls eggs from the cliffs and sent them off to Glasgow and London. On Sundays, with his Bible in his hand, he walked through the fields to attend morning service in the church. He became friendly with three different ministers during his time there, and often had a dram and played chess with one of them.

About 1936 he became ill and was taken to Maud hospital. He died a few weeks later. 'For some fifteen years in this small sheltered spot he lived his lonely life,' wrote Mary, 'and now fifty years later as I look down on that same spot I can see so little trace. The cave is empty, but the stones he built to shelter still lie around; no trace of his garden, yet the small stream that gave it nourishment still flows towards the sea. The sea and the scenery the same, as are the cries of the seagulls mingled with the murmur of water as it gently laps the shore, which could change so quickly to the angry sound of waves breaking on the boulders. How he came to this cave on Aberdour shore and made it his own we will never know.'

I left Mary and her memories of the Hermit and followed the old coach road to Pennan. The scenery changes, softly and subtly at first, as you go towards Banffshire, and here and there roads detach themselves and go plunging down to picturesque little villages that have one foot in the sea and one on the land. The writer Peter Anson thought that Penan was the most picturesque community; after a series of grey villages all the way up the coast, he said, it was difficult to accustom yourself to a village where everything was red — 'a warm, purple red, almost crimson, red houses, red roads, red cliffs, red beach, red rocks.' Now, of course, another red has been added to Pennan's colourful image, for down on the sea front, outside the local hotel, there is a well-known tourist attraction — the red telephone booth which became a 'prop' in the Bill Forsyth film *Local Hero*, starring Burt Lancaster.

Pennan is on the east side of Troup Head, but another village which wages endless war against the sea is Crovie (pronounced Crivie), on the west side. It is the smallest of Buchan's bottom-of-the-cliff villages, its long row of cottages split by a burn running down from the headland. The gable ends of most of the houses face on to the sea, while the other ends bury themselves in the cliff face. Nearly a century and a half ago, a Gamrie schoolmaster, Alexander Whyte, said that they were 'like a brood of young seafowl nestling with their heads under the dam.' There were about a hundred fishermen in this tiny village last century, and in 1881 Crovie could boast as many as sixty fishing boats. Today they are all gone, for Crovie lost the battle against the sea in the great storm of 1953, which resulted in many of the fishers quitting the village for Gardenstown.

Crovie and Pennan are the 'seafowls,' and the arrogant snout of Troup Head is the 'dam.' With its scarred and riven cliffs, the Pennan side of this magnificent headland is the most impressive. Here, at Cullykhan Bay, a subterranean passage under a rock called the Needle's E'e leads to a cave known as the Devil's Diningroom. Another promontory, the Lion's Head, is breached by a huge, 50 ft. deep fissure called Hell's Lum. In the past, visitors flocked to Troup Head to see spume erupting through this gash in the land. It got the name Hells' Lum because from the distance the blown spindthrift made it look a smoking chimney. 'It is,' wrote one observer, 'a ghastly spot.'

For me, however, hell lay in another part of this stormy North-east coast — and the Devil was waiting not many miles away.

CHAPTER EIGHT
The Pits of Hell

Salvation and damnation stalk each other along the ragged seaboard of the Moray Firth. Between Kinnaird Head and Rosehearty are the Three Pits of Hell, while farther west the twin horns of the De'il rise above the chimney pots of Buckie. Here, if you put your ear to the past, you can listen to the boom and blast of the Sally Ann bands as they go marching through the fisher towns, or hear the voices of the old-time evangelists calling on sinners to come and be saved.

Yet things are not always as they seem. There was no sniff of brimstone when I travelled along this stretch of the North-east coast, for the three Pitsof Hell were Pittullie, Pittendrum and Pitsligo, quiet, peaceful places, yet damned as an unholy Trinity by a sour-tongued minister after Pitsligo had broken away from the parish of Aberdour in 1633. As for the De'il's horns, that was the name given to the twin spires of St Peter's Roman Catholic Church by someone else with a misplaced sense of humour.

The Devil may be gone from Buckie, but the 'cockie-coo' still lurks in its memory, if not in its back-streets. This was a strange beastie that local fishermen believed waited for them in the mornings so that it could seize hold of their bonnets when they left their homes to go to sea. Although religion has always played an important part in their lives, superstition was its pagan partner. The revivalists shouted out the message that Christ was their Skipper, the Holy Spirit their Pilot, and that God himself was at the helm, yet, paradoxically, even the most religious fisherman thought it unlucky if he met a minister on the way to his boat.

There were names and words that were taboo, and still are to-day. Fishermen never mentioned the word 'salmon;' instead, they spoke about red fish or scaly fish. Flat-footed people were regarded as 'ill-fitted,' or unlucky, and in Portknockie even dogs were looked upon as ill omens. Nairn fishermen avoided shooting nets on the port side because it brought bad luck, and they refused to taste food before any fish were caught. The words 'pig' or 'swine' were shunned. One minister emptied his church by talking about 'the husks that the swine did eat.'

When a great religious revival swept through the east coast of Scotland in the second half of last century,it nurtured a staggering number of religious groups and sects. The majority of fishermen in the North-east were Presbyterian, but alongside them were the Baptists, who were either 'Strict' or 'Particular,' and the Brethren, whose organisation split into two in 1848, leaving it with the Plymouth or Open Brethren on one side and the Exclusive or Close Brethren on the other. The Close Brethren's narrow interpretation of Biblical edicts was to lead to bitterness and broken homes.

There were other, smaller groups who, finding little to satisfy them in any of the major movements, broke off and worshipped in their own gospel halls. At one time there were at least twelve different religious denominations in Findochty. The meeting places of three of them can still be seen at the end of Chapel Street, two of them, a Salvation Army building and a Plymouth Brethren hall, in bright coats of blue and white. The Brethren hall was originally a smiddy, with the upper floor used as a loft for drying nets. In the street above, almost on top of them, is the sober frontage of the Methodist church.

There were few Catholic or Episcopalian fisher families on the east coast of Scotland. Most of those who belonged to the Catholic faith were in Buckie, but the strength of the Catholic church lay in its hinterland, in Gordon country. Go three miles inland to the Braes of Enzie and you are taking the pulse of Catholicism. 'This Country is inhabited entirely by Papists, whom the family of Gordon retain here, thinking they pay higher rents than any one else would,' wrote Alexander Carlyle in 1765. In 1617 there were over one thousand Catholics in Banffshire. In the heart of the rich Enzie farmland there is a large R.C. burial ground, St Ninian's, which is known as Banffshire's Bethlehem. It stands on the site of an earlier chapel.

In this land of gentle braes and 'bonnie ferms' the names have 'a lilt an' a sough like a lang-kept tune,' as J. M. Caie put it in his poem, 'The Enzie.' He ran a roll-call on the 'bonnie ferms' — Birkenbush, Sauchenbush, Cowfurrach, Oran, Cuttlebrae, Auchentae, Preshome, Dallachy, Gollachy, and a few more.

I saw them on the road signs as I wandered about the Braes of Enzie, 'a curnie daft aul--farrant wirds tae them that doesna ken,' but I never came across the Smerick or the Cockhat Kirk — 'a queer name thon,' said Caie. One of the verses went —

There's Dallachy an' Gollachy,
   Wellheads an' Allalath,
The sand road tae Clochan, an'
   Whiteash's strait wee path.

The road to Clochan, no longer a sand road, leads to St Gregory's Chapel, Preshome, a large, cathedral-like building, dating from 1788, that looks as if it would be more at home among city streets than in the back of beyond at Enzie. Yet Preshome, which began as a heather-thatched cottage where Bishop Thomas Nicholson lived at the end of the 17th century, has played an important part in the life of the Catholic Church in Scotland, although in recent years it had gone into decline. Mrs Isobel McPherson, who lives in the Chapelhouse, found a piece of paper stuck under a door to stop draughts. It was a list of communicants in 1829, and there were 1400 names on it. Now, she told me, only a handful of people turn up for worship.

At Tynet, less than two miles away, there is another Catholic church, St Ninian, which also began its life as a cottage, and it is still one to-day. The laird of Tynet offered it to the Catholic community of Enzie in 1755, and it is believed to be the oldest post-Reformation R.C. Church in Scotland — I have heard it called Banffshire's Bethlehem. Its whitewashed walls hide an impressive interior, for it was beautifully restored in 1951, and to-day it holds regular Saturday night services.

Enzie is full of wonders, not least being a curious double-storey 18th century bridge over the Burn of Buckie. The original bridge, built low over the burn, was used by pack horses, but when it was found to be unsuitable for carriages another bridge was built on top of it. This architectural folly is near Drybridge, a tiny hamlet full of old-world charm. It houses cluster around a red-roofed smiddy built in 1777. George Duncan, who died over two years ago, was Drybridge's last blacksmith; now his son, Alan, runs it as an antique business, dispatching huge containers of antiques to America. Alan's mother, Mrs Sheila Duncan, is the local postmistress.

While Catholicism flourished on the Braes of Enzie, the fishing communities along the Moray Firth coast were moving towards their own salvation. The middle of the 19th century brought the Great Revival, or, rather, a series of revivals, with Methodists, Baptists, Brethren, and the Salvation Army all reaching out for the souls of the fishers.

James Turner was the man who lit the fire. This Peterhead cooper and herring curer, who turned to Methodism after many years as a Presbyterian, was excommunicated by the Kirk for being bold enough or foolish enough to pray for the conversion of unenlightened ministers. He preached his first sermon in Collieston in 1854, and in 1859, the year of the Great Revival, began to extend his activities, holding religious meetings in a number of Buchan fishing villages, and even going farther afield to Aberdeen, Dundee and Perth.

'Jeems' Turner became the Billy Graham of his time. His church was his family's fish-curing shed, with gutting troughs on one side and coopers' benches on the other. The congregation sat on planks and fish barrels, and the atmosphere was thick with the smoke and smell of salt fish and oil lamps. He opened a Banffshire mission at Cullen in 1860, but collapsed while preaching at Cornhill. When he died two years later it was estimated that he had converted more than 8000 people along the North-east coast.

In retrospect, some regarded the religious revival with a degree of scepticism. In *Behold Thy Daughter*, the novelist Neil Paterson, who was brought up in Banff, described it as 'a form of insanity' and said that it brought a sharp rise in the birth-rate. 'Hundreds were struck down dramatically in swoons, and there was hardly a family on the coast from Collieston to

Clyth in which there was not at least one case of mental or physical prostration.'

Yet Turner sent out a call that was to ring down through the years. The revival of 1859 was followed by the appearance of the Salvation Army, who held a strong appeal for the fishing folk, and behind them came the Baptists, setting up 'bethels' and meeting houses in almost every fishing village on the Moray Firth coast. Then, in 1921, during the autumn fishing season at Yarmouth and Lowestoft, another Great Revival sent a tidal wave of religious fervour through the Scottish fishing communities.

This time, the preacher was a young fisherman called Dave Cordiner, tall, with jet-black hair and a dynamism that drew huge crowds to his meetings. He preached in the open air, at street corners and under lamposts. His congregation of fishermen and fisher girls sang hymns and listened to converted 'brothers' describing their spiritual awakening, and the night air rang to the sound of 'Hallelujahs.' Cordiner's successor was another cooper, Jock Troup, a Wick man, and his friend Wullie Bruce, who ran an evangelical campaign that was reminiscent of Moody and Sankey in the previous century.

The Poet of Portsoy remembers these soul-stirring days. Jim Slater, who became a fisherman in 1917 and is now 87 years old, has written a number of books on fishing and fishermen, many of them in verse. I sat with him in his home near the Shore head in Portsoy and talked about the old days. He showed me a poem he had written called 'Satan's Claim Refuted' —

I've heard a tale, it micht be true,
It may be you hae heard it too,
That Satan on his evil way
Once viewed Portsoy frae Langie's Brae,
And lookin' doon wi' evil glee
He said, 'I'll hae ye a' wi' me.'

Jim was snatched from Auld Nick's horny grasp during the Great Revival of the 1920s. He remembers vividly how the events at Great Yarmouth reached back to the fishing villages on the Moray Firth. Jock Troup was a member of the Salvation

Army, and during the Yarmouth fishing a Charabanc Crusade of Salvationists descended on East Anglia. On their return from the English port the Sally Ann evangelists continued their campaign. Jim himself became a Salvationist after a meeting on the Shorehead. He wrote about it in one of his poems —

It was in nineteen twenty-three the
  'Army' cam' along,
And on the Shorehead preached the word
  and sang salvation's song;
God blessed the message, simply told,
  I still can mind it fine
For on that day wi' ither lads I made
  the Saviour mine.

The Public Hall in Portsoy Square was the Salvation Army headquarters. It was known as Adam Minty's Hall.

The year o' seventeen ninety eight is
  cut out on the wall
And lang ago this place was kent
  as Adam Minty's Hall
He carried on a business there in
  wines o' every grade,
And so this hall took on that name
  because o' Minty's trade.

The date 1798 can still be seen on the wall of Adam Minty's wine shop, but the Sally Ann has long since departed. 'The only Salvationist that can be seen here,' says Jim, 'are those who come from along the coast to visit the local hospitals.' The hall is now used by Jehovah Witnesses.

Jim Slater is no fanatical 'Bible-thumper,' so it is interesting to look at the reasons for his conversion. His parents were members of the Church of Scotland, and on the day he was 'saved' he had been to morning service. He felt there was something lacking. 'There was no power in the message,' he said. 'It was the usual dull sermon.' Nearly seventy years later, the same sort of criticism is still being levelled at the Kirk, but to-day there are no fiery evangelists stomping the land to bring the people back to prayer. The notices can still be seen outside the meeting houses — 'If the Lord will the word of God will be preached in this room on the Lord's Day' — but few people answer the call.

Some, however, still carry on, preaching to pitifully small congregations. Jim McKay, a retired fisherman, is leader of the Plymouth Brethren in tiny Sandend. Their meeting place is the old village school. There was a time when you would have been lucky to get into the hall for a service, let alone get a seat; people perched on window-sills to sing their hymns and say their prayers.

That was in the days when there were 250 people in the Assembly in Sandend, compared with a handful to-day. Sylvia McKay remembers when the Gospel Hall was full of people. Now, she says, God doesn't come into their lives. Her husband, Jim, was a fisherman until 1968, and an insurance agent until he retired four years ago. Although he is a member of the Plymouth Brethren, he would prefer to be known 'just as a Christian.'

Perhaps this has something to do with the kind of mythology that has grown up around the Brethren. The Sandend movement is 'Open,' and Jim McKay says there are no rules and regulations, no do's and don'ts. He hasn't got a television set, but no one told him not to have one; he just thinks there is 'too much evil on it.' If someone tries to sell him a raffle ticket he won't take it, but he will give a donation to whatever cause it will benefit.

The first meeting in Sandend was in a garret at No. 37. There are no official records, but it is thought that his visit took place in 1893, the year that James McKendrick, one of the great 19th century evangelists, preached in the North-east. He came up through Gourdon, where the fisher folks seldom went to church; called in at Boddam, which had the most unruly congregation he had ever seen (when he was preaching the young men were busy tying the women's shawls together around the backs of their seats); and preached at Findochty, which had been visited by 'the saintly James Turner' and was slipping back into drunkenness.

McKendrick held his meeting in the school, but many people were unable to get in. Next year, while in Portknockie, the evangelist went back to Sandend to meet some of his old friends, among them John and George Innes, who lived at No. 37. They broke bread in their cramped garret and one of them told McKendrick, 'We will pray for you as long as we live.' He had no idea how short a time that would be.

There were four Innes brothers, and the following Saturday they were at sea when a furious gale blew up, lashing the Moray Firth coast. Other boats were able to reach the harbour, but the people on shore watched in vain for the return of the Innes brothers. They had been fishing only four miles from the shore, but their boat foundered. All four perished, leaving behind four widows and fourteen orphans, as well as an aged father and mother who depended on them.

Standing outside the Gospel Hall, Jim McKay looks across Sandend Bay to where the Innes brothers went to their doom. He sometimes preaches there, out in the open; at other times, he gathers a congregation about him at the harbour, at the end of his close, or on the road above the bay, carrying on a tradition set more than a century ago by fishermen like 'Jeems' Turner and Dave Cordiner. A good deal of myth and mystery has surrounded the activities of the Brethren over the years, aggravated by controversy over the Exclusive Brethren, but Jim and Sylvia McKay uphold the beliefs of a dwindling corps of evangelists by talking openly and honestly about their faith.

Just south of the coast road from Macduff to Rosehearty there is a farm with the chilling name of Bloodymyre. It is said to mark the site of the Battle of the Bloody Pits in 1004, when an army of invading Danes was routed. A few miles to the east is another link with the battle, the ruined Church of St John the Evangelist. The shell of the chapel sits on the lofty heights of Gamrie Mhor, where the skulls of dead Danes were taken after the battle. At one time, you would have seen them leering at you from the wall of the church, for in 1832, a visitor wrote about the Norsemen's skulls 'grinning horrid and hollow' near the pulpit.

Tumbling tombstones lie about this old kirkyard, which has a spectacular view across Gamrie Bay to where the red-clay cliffs drop down to the Seatown of Gardenstown. Beyond it,

Crovie keeps a fragile hold on the land. They say that people used to carry coffins along the shore and up the steep braes to the kirkyard. Until the second half of the 18th century, Macduff folk going to Sunday worship had to walk seven miles to St John's, which was their parish church.

Gamrie was the old name for Gardenstown, and some people still call it that. The writer Peter Anson thought that its inhabitants were 'a different race,' and if that is still true it is easy to see why. One reason is its setting. Crovie, its near neighbour, lodged itself nervously at the foot of the cliffs, but Gardenstown decided to climb up them and rejoin the outside world, building its houses on a series of narrow terraces linked by winding braes, or, as Gamrie schoolmaster Alexander Whyte put it, 'a winding footpath like a staircase, on which few can venture without fear and trembling.'

Nowadays, the fear and trembling are likely to be induced by cars. Gardenstown is a motorist's nightmare, although local drivers, particularly the young, go down its plunging streets as if they were on some carnival helter-skelter. To avoid them, fearful pedestrians can walk down stone steps that have been cut out of the cliff face. Entering the village from the Macduff road you go through the modern Gardenstown, with expensive houses and expensive cars at their doors, the financial 'harvest' of fishing's boom years. That is another thing that sets them apart from other fishing villages — Gardenstown has been described as the wealthiest village in Scotland.

The third reason for Gamrie folk being 'a different race' is the fact that Gardenstown is, or was, a stronghold of the Brethren movement, both Exclusive and Open. Its link with the Brethren put it unwillingly under the spotlight in 1954 when two men appeared in court charged with conducting themselves in a disorderly manner at the Garden Arms Hotel by cursing and swearing and using indecent language. The words were 'damn' and 'bloody' and the charges were found 'Not Proven.'

Families in Gardenstown have always been more closely-knit than in other villages, which probably has something to do with the houses being built practically on top of each other. Norman Tennant, the hotel proprietor at the time of the swearing case, said that neighbours were so close to each other that they hardly needed to raise their voices. So it was not surprising that the Brethren in Gardenstown were the first to reject the harsh edicts of 'Big Jim' Taylor, the American leader of the Exclusive Brethren, whose attitude to unbelievers and 'Separate Tables' broke up countless families.

To-day, the movement is on the decline, but religion is still strong in this cliff-hanging community on the Banffshire coast. On the day that I was there — a Sunday — cars were parked tail-to-bumper down the steep brae. Their owners were not crowding the Brethren halls; they were attending the church of Scotland service. Its notice board proclaims its creed as 'Evangelical and Reform.'

Perhaps the young are changing things. Down on the quay, I saw a group of them flaunting their flashy cars, smoking, trying to impress their girl-friends, and showing a general air of bravado. One youth roared on to the quay, braked and did a ninety degree turn in his vehicle, throwing up great clouds of dust as he came to a halt perilously near the harbour wall.

I wondered what the evangelist James McKendrick would have said. He preached in a fish-curing shed in Gardenstown, using a fish box as his platform. The Salvation Army had already tried to hold meetings in the village, but had given up because of a group of young troublemakers. They were there when McKendrick climbed on to his fish box. When they began to laugh and jeer, he asked them to be quiet. Finally, as the rowdyism continued, he pushed his way into the crowd, grabbed the ring-leader by the scruff of the neck, and threw him out of the building. There was no more trouble.

I couldn't help thinking that a McKendrick or a 'Jeems' Turner might have taken some of the brashness out of the youngsters parading on the quayside at Gardenstown.

CHAPTER NINE
'Gweed Saut Water'

When the folk of Banff look across Banff Bay to the tall, domed clock tower of Macduff's Doune Church, they see a blank face where the clock should be. It all goes back to the time when Banff itself meddled with one of its clocks. In 1700, when the Highland freebooter James McPherson was strung up on the gallows at Banff's Mercat Cross, the town's clock was put forward an hour to ensure that he was executed before the arrival of a last-minute pardon. The Macduff townsfolk were so incensed by this that they built their church with an empty clock face so that their neighbours across the water would never know the right time again.

That, at anyrate, is the story, officially approved for tourist consumption, and for all we know it may be true, for MacPherson was regarded as a bit of a Robin Hood. Nevertheless, it becomes slightly suspect when you think that Macduff must have nursed its sense of outrage for more than a century before getting its own back. Doune Church was built in 1805.

On the other hand, it may have had something to do with the age-old rivalry between the two burghs. Banff and Macduff are Siamese-twin towns, locked together by a seven-arched bridge over the River Deveron, yet they have little in common. Banff, with its ancient history and abundance of historic buildings, has an air of genteel superiority, as if well aware that the county's gentry once had their elegant town houses in the 'the gayest little town in Scotland.' Byron spent his schoolboy holidays with his grandmother at a house called Little Fillicap in Low Street, and Dr Samuel Johnson and James Boswell spent a night in the Black Bull Inn in 1773.

The Black Bull, which was replaced by the Fife Arms Hotel, was dismissed as 'indifferent' by the happy travellers, but the doctor may have been piqued by the fact that the Earl of Fife was not at home in his baroque mansion at Duff House. 'We should have had a very elegant reception from his lordship,' said Boswell. In 1906, Duff House was donated jointly to Banff and Macduff, but most people have always regarded it as belonging to Banff. In 1956, it was handed over to the Department of Environment.

Now Banff is to enjoy a piece of cultural one-upmanship. Duff House has been more or less an empty shell in recent years, with people paying to walk through its bare rooms while thinking of its historic past, but a decision has been taken to turn the Adam mansion into an outpost of the Scottish National Gallery in Edinburgh. From its walls will hang paintings appropriate to a country house of its era, and the feeling is that it will become a tourist attraction of national importance, drawing visitors from all over Britain as well as abroad.

Meanwhile, Macduff goes its own way. The seatown was originally called Doune, and at one time the plan was to call the burgh Douneduff, but it was thought that this was dangerously near 'Doon wi' the Duffs!,' which wouldn't have gone down well with the head of the Duff family, the second Earl of Fife. Macduff may not have had Dr Johnson, but it had Dr Walford Bodie, the Wizard of the North, with his waxed moustache and piercing eyes, who hypnotised his patrons, made ladies vanish into space, and was hailed as the Wonder of the World. Macduff was his adopted town (he was Aberdeen-born) and he lived in the Manor House in Skene Street. He had Macduff's interests at heart, and he built a Bath House and swimming pool on the foreshore along High Shore.

It seems as if cleanliness, inner *and* outer, was a passion with the people of Macduff last century, for as well as enjoying mineral water from the Well of Tarlair they went in for sea-bathing and *drinking* sea water. 'Gweed, clean saut water,' said Maister Saun'ers from Marnoch, in William Alexander's classic book, *Johnny Gibb of Gushetneuk.* When Widow Will's son, Jock, said it would make him spew, he was told, 'Ye sud gae at it hardier an' ye wud never think aboot the taste o' it.' Poor Will was also encouraged to eat dulse – 'a very halesome thing ta'en wi' the water.'

The virtues of the Wells at Tarlair were also extolled in Alexander's Doric novel. The water cured everything from 'scabbit faces' to 'sair een,' and every year, after he had got the 'neeps doon,' Johnny would take his carts to the mill-dam, scrub off the "neep muck,' and set off with a party on an annual pilgrimage to Tarlair. That was in 1839; a century later the flow of water was cut off when a mine blew up after being washed ashore. The bathing still goes on, although in less chilling conditions, but no one drinks Maister Saun'ers' 'gweed, clean halesome water' any more.

There could never have been 'neep muck' or any other muck in Banff, for it was once praised as 'a perfect model of cleanliness,' but across the Deveron you were liable to catch your breath as you sniffed what the Buchan poet Flora Garry called 'the caller guff o' tar an' raips an' dilse alang the sea-wynds o' Macduff.' Up on the Hill of Doune a huge ship's anchor stands in the shadow of the church. Dragged up in the nets of a local fishing boat, it is 13ft. long and weighs more than 3 tons. It is believed to be from an 18th century sailing ship, and now it stands beside the Market Cross as a symbol of the town's long association with the sea.

Although Banff was once an importance centre of shipping, and later a busy herring port, it went into decline when its harbour silted up. Macduff, on the other hand, prospered. From the anchor on the Hill of Doune, looking down on a harbour that was said to be one of the best on the Moray Firth, I tried to work out where Harbour Head would have been before a new fishmarket and ice factory were built. For fourteen years, Harbour Head was the home of Peter Anson, the writer and artist, a Southsea man who made his home among the North-east fishers and became an outstanding authority on fishing and fisherfolk. It was at Harbour Head, a low-roofed, one-storey cottage on Low Shore, that he produced many of his books and sketches, compiling over the years a remarkable record of the Scottish fishing industry.

When he moved into the cottage he had no electricity, no water, and scarcely any light from the three small windows. It was a rough and ready existence, yet Anson was happy there.

He got on well with the fishermen – 'They never treated me as an incomer or a stranger, but always as a friend,' he said – and his home became a meeting place for local 'loons,' youngsters with names like Stutters, Touzan, Beastie, Curly and Buzzer. They were known as the Harbour Head Gang.

Anson, born in 1889, was a deeply religious man. He joined an Anglican Benedictine community on Caldey Island in 1910 and in 1921 went for a time to a monastery at Fort Augustus. That was the year of the great East Coast religious revival, and Anson witnessed it himself when he was in Great Yarmouth writing and sketching. He saw groups of fishermen 'listening with hungry, eager faces to the fiery, passionate words of some young evangelist,' and saw weather-beaten skippers and young deckhands making their way to the 'Penitents' Form.'

When he was living at Harbour Head he turned his loft into a chapel. Priests staying with him celebrated Mass there. 'On a summer morning,' he wrote, 'when the skylights were open, the mutter of Latin mingled with the murmur of the waves. The harsh cries of gulls, against a background of the rattle of the winch and derrick of a coaster discharging coal or lime, made music that was maritime if not strictly liturgical.'

In the late 1960s, while living at Ferryden, Montrose, he began work on a 'panorama' of the Scottish fishing industry, hoping that one day there would be a museum on the Moray Firth coast which would display it. If his cottage on the Low Shore had been retained and restored, Harbour Head might have housed the 'panorama,' but it was demolished in 1974, the year before his death. As it was, 400 of his watercolours were presented to the newly-opened Buckie Maritime Museum in 1973, followed by a further sixteen just before his death.

Anson knew Buckie well. He travelled along this stretch of Banff coast sketching and painting Findochty and the three 'ports' – Portknockie and Portessie to the east of Buckie, and Portgordon to the west. Portgordon was originally called Gollachy, and there is still a Gollachy Ice House, although it is unused and in a bad state of repair.

From Portessie, you sweep towards Buckie along the grandly-named Great Eastern Road. Portessie has a liking for fancy names, for I spotted a corner of the village called Vanity Fair, and the village itself has had three names. It was known at one time as Rottinslough, and even to-day people talk about 'The Sloch,' and then it became Porteasy. Now, it seems, they have settled for the name Portessie.

Peter Anson said that few towns in Scotland were so utterly dependent upon the sea as Buckie. He was talking of a time when 200 steam drifters 'squeezed together like sardines in the basins with little or no room between them.' In *Fishing Boats and Fisher Folk on the East Coast of Scotland,* he looked back to the time when Buckie lads went to sea at the age of fourteen and married at eighteen, and when women carried their husbands to their boats so that they wouldn't get their feet wet before going to sea.

'Fishermen's marriages in Buckie must have been wonderful affairs,' he wrote. 'Previous to the ceremony the kirk session exacted a pledge of half a guinea that no rioting or fighting would take place. If, as a result of too much whisky having been consumed, there was brawling or even bloodshed, the pledge was given to the poor, but if the party managed to behave itself the money was returned to the bridegroom the following Sabbath.'

He wrote about the fishers' pay, their looks (both men and women were 'remarkably stout and well-shaped'), and their food at sea (barley meal, bannocks, roast haddocks and a pint of kail), and he declared: 'Such was fisher-life in Buckie in the old days.'

But, as well as dipping into the more distant past, Anson used pen and paintbrush to draw a vivid picture of his own era. The material he left behind, his sketches, paint-ings and books, and a collection of over 2000 photographs, postcards, prints, newspaper cuttings and drawings, ensured that the 'old days' never be forgotten, for it added up to a vast storehouse of information about the Scottish fishing industry.

Now, in addition to holding and displaying many of his drawings and watercolours, Buckie is continuing the tradition set by Peter Anson. In 1990, the Buckie and District Fishing

Heritage Society, whose aim is to create a record of the fishing and ancillary industries along the Banffshire coast, opened new premises behind the Town House in Cluny Place. Here, they are building a picture of what life was like in this fishing community many years ago.

There is not much space in the society's two rooms, but Jim Merson, the secretary, makes the best of what he has, for the walls are crowded with old photographs, maps and models. There are badges from the funnel of a drifter, coopers' tools, tackle, creels used by fisher girls, and many other exhibits.

At the other end of the town, members of an employment training programme have been helping the Heritage Centre by gathering information and photographs about fisher life in Buckie. Jan Pennington, the training supervisor, showed me a scrapbook kept by George Slater, a local shipbuilder, who jotted down notes on anything that interested him . . . information about fishing boats, sketches of ropes and knots, drawings of Scaffies, a flashback to the great gale of 1848, and a reminder of the terrible Stotfield disaster on Christmas Day, 1806, when three Lossiemouth boats, with twenty one men on board, were lost in a sudden storm. The result was that seventeen widows, forty-seven children and eight aged parents were left destitute.

Fishing communities live with the fear of such disasters. There is a poignant reminder of this in a chapel in Buckie's New Street, built in memory of all those who have lost their lives at sea since 1945. The stained glass windows were made by a local artist, Charles Florence. It is a quiet, beautiful place, but sad.

A good deal of the material at the Heritage Centre is connected with sea dramas. There is a poem written in 1893 by a Nathan Smith after a fishing boat, the *Jessie Smith* – a Zulu – sank with nine men on board in February of that year. Three brothers, John, William and Joseph Boggen, each with the middle name Smith, were lost, and a father and son, both named Alexander Clark, were among those drowned.

It may not be great poetry, but it is a stark record of what happened to that frail little craft and its crew on a Tuesday morning, 'black and grim,' on the 14th of February, 1893. Nathan Smith, who must have seen the Zulu set out on its last voyage, described how members of the crew waved to their children as they left Buckie harbour 'to fish for cod in Northern Bay.' Forty miles from the shore, they were hit by a sudden squall –

The *Jessie Smith* had reefed her sails
When caught amid that fearful gale,
They hoist the mizzen for the shore,
Alas, that place they'll see no more.

The crew of another fishing boat saw the vessel being engulfed by huge seas. It was, said Nathan Smith, 'just like a midnight dream.'

More sea tragedies are recorded in newspaper cuttings and other accounts held by the Heritage Centre. In August, 1885, the *Banffshire Advertiser* reported on a gale of hurricane force that had disastrous consequences for North-east fishing fleets. On that day, 500 boats from Fraserburgh alone put to sea. From Aberdeen to Burghead, many boats were lost, and their crews with them.

The tales are endless ... a Findochty skipper being lashed to his seat by his crew during a storm, a Portknockie boat swamped three miles from the shore with the loss of five men, a Buckie boat sticking at the entrance to Cullen harbour and ending up as a total wreck, and a sea boot being found on the sands at Cullen with a man's foot in it. The stocking on the foot was identified by a Portknockie woman as her husband's. He was drowned with four other fishermen when their boat capsized in 1887.

But it is not all gloom and doom. George Slater's notebook yielded up a poem in praise of the hard-working fisher girls, who had laughter on their lips and 'brine and pickle on their tongues.' They had become 'slaves to short-arsed curers' in England, but they had 'a sprinkling of pride on their hearts, keeping them sound.' They could look after themselves, for their sharp North-east tongues were a match for anyone – 'their tongues' gutting knife,' said the poet, 'would tear a strip from the Lowlander's mockery.'

Salt the reward they won
from thousands of barrels.
And the burden of poverty in their kists,
And were it not for their laughter
you might think the harp string
was broken.

Perhaps the most satisfying part of the Heritage Centre's work is the compiling of oral tapes, interviews with retired fishermen like seventy-year-old John Murray, who went to sea in 1936 and retired six years ago. There were, in fact, two John Murrays on this particular tape, one John from Titness Street, who was identified by his T-name, 'Bodge,' and a second John from the Yardie, who is known as 'Smacker.'

So it was the 'Bodge and Smacker' show, presented in broad Doric. It began with the names of their first boats – the *Forelock* and the *Fruitful* – and a description of working conditions in the old days –

'In steam days ye hid a chief an' a fireman, that's a' that ye hid. The fireman got aboot 30/- a week, an' the engineer got aboot £2, aye £2 10/-. They had different size o' engines ye see. There wis compound engines and triple engines. That wis the bigger size, the triple engines. But they were a' steam, they hid tae shuffle in the coal intae the biler tae get the steam up tae get the engine tae go ye see. The skipper jist rang doon whit he winted at the telegraph. The fireman took her to sea an' the chief took her ashore. Wi' nine men, aye in the fishin' days.'

Before they sailed at start of the fishing season the boat had to be painted, the ropes tarred, and the nets taken out of store. Then the equipment and groceries had to be collected –

'Ye gid roon' the hale toon wi' a horse an' cairt in they days, aye, Geordie Milton's. Ye gid roon a' the crew, maybe nine o' a crew, in the summertime, an' ye got a' his gear aboard, his beddie an' his blankets an' his oilskins an' beets, an' then ye finished up at the grocer's afore ye gid doon. An' ye took a' yer, weel, a bagfu' o' sugar in those days min', a hunnerweight bag, an' a great big box o' butter dip, it wis in half puns, ye ken, twenty-eight pun boxes, and fit else, tea. It wis in three ply wid boxes, wis it three pun boxes? I canna min'. An' ye hid boxes o' prunes an' boxes o' dried fruit, apple rings, an' a thingmart o' cheese, ane o' that great big roon' anes, ye ken. Aye, nae the wee roon' anes, ane o' the big anes. Ye used tae slice aff a bit. . .'

The fishermen usually had fried herring for breakfast, sometimes nearly three dozen of them, depending on the size. If they had a good cook it was all right, but some of the cooks were barely out of school and knew little about the culinary arts, even in a drifter's galley. When the two Johns first went to sea they were only fourteen years old – and *they* were the cooks. There were a lot of teenage cooks. Some were good at it and stayed in the galley, but others took the job simply with the aim of getting on the deck.

The weather forecasts were picked up twice a day on a wireless set that was 'jist a box wi' a weet battery an' a dry battery,' but the 'auld lads' could tell the weather by looking at the sky or watching the birds. They knew that a red sky at night meant good weather, but a red sky in the morning didn't bother them as much as a *green* sky. 'In the sail boat days they didna' like tae see a pea green sky in the mornin'. That wis a gale o' win' – a sign o' win'.'

When Badger and Smacker were discussing pea green skies and weather forecasts, there was a problem about T-names. George Cowie was mentioned as the authority on pea green skies, but Buckie is full of Cowies. The question arose – which George Cowie? The conversation that followed might have come straight from a 'Scotland the What?' script.

Wis that 'Codlin'?
No, 'Pum'. George 'Pum'.
I ken George Cowie 'Codlin'.
Wha wis he?
Fae Gordon Street.
Is that him that wis in the factory?

Mhum.
He wis niver at the sea.
No, bit he got it fae his father he said. He wis usually
    accurate wi' his weather forecasts.
I widna thocht that noo.
No, bit he is.
*I widna thocht 'Codlin' himsel' wid hae been onything. He
    wis a deckie wi' ma father. Maybe he wid a'
    repeated whit he heard ither lads sayin'.*
Aye, that's fit I'm sayin'.

Bodge and Smacker had a lengthy discussion on superstition.
Some lads, they said, would never sail on a Friday – 'They sail
ony time noo.' Black was a forbidden colour; if a fisherman
saw a black cat he would turn back. Telling the time was also
frowned on.

'I'll tell ye fit happened tae his ainse, this wis in Yarmooth
an' this wis aefter the war. This lad wis awfa' superstitious, of
course Buckpool is awfa' superstitious, an' we wis gan' doon
the river ay Sunday mornin' an' there wis a Gamrie boat comes
up oor starn, an' he says 'Fit time es't?' an' I tell't him fit time
it wis an' I happened tae say fin' I geed ootside, an' they caw'd
me athin'. Aye, they said ye winna see a herrin' the hale week
an by ... we didna. We niver got a herrin' the whole bloomin'
week till Friday.'

One of the veterans told the interviewer that he took 'a
dose o' shirts in a bag' when he went to sea, but some of
the older fishermen were less fastidious; they 'nivver shifted
for a month.' Cooks and firemen were always having a wash
– 'jist in a bucket like.'

If you went to Stornoway you could get a shower in the local
mission, but that was after the war. Before the war there was
nothing. The only place open in Stornoway on a Sunday was a
'shoppie' run by a woman called 'Fool' Maggie – 'She wis that
'fool' (dirty), we caw'd her 'Fool' Maggie.'

Bodge and Smacker talked about characters like 'Fool' Maggie, about pay and conditions on the old drifters, and about the
'quines' who went down to Yarmouth with them. They spoke
about 'Codlin' Cowie and skippers like Christmas Charlie, 'a lad
in the Broch,' who was given his nickname because 'he nivver

came oot o' Yarmooth till Christmas time every year,' and they opened up a window on a world that has almost completely disappeared.

Buckie may look to the future, but it cherishes its past. When I was at the Heritage Centre, a feasability study was being carried out on the possibility of having a bigger centre. The obvious place for it would be the harbour. I hope it comes about, for Jim Merson and his helpers are doing a magnificent job. Moreover, it would be nice to think that Bodge and Smacker will continue to tell their salty tales to future generations of Buckie folk.

CHAPTER TEN
Katie's Teenie's Bobby

The little boat bounced across the bay towards the row of jagged rocks that marked the entrance to Sandend harbour. Bob Bruce, the owner, pointed to a two-storey building dominating the cluster of cottages on the quayside. 'Take your line from the drainpipe on the Muckle Hoose,' he said. So, with this unorthodox navigational aid to guide me, and keeping one eye on the spot where a rock called the Stane lurked under the water, I steered the *Toby* into Scotland's smallest fishing port.

The Muckle Hoose, a former watch house, didn't let me down, but as the 16ft motor boat eased its way into the harbour I remembered a photograph I had seen hanging on the wall of an upstairs room in Bob's house in Sandend. It showed a group of people standing on the quay, among them a white-bearded fisherman in waistcoat and bonnet, hands in pockets, taking stock of what was going on. He was Bob's grandfather, Willie Smith, and I thought to myself that if he was looking down from some watery Valhalla he would probably be wondering what Katy's Teenie's Bobby was up to.

Katy was Bob Bruce's grandmother and Teenie (Christina) his mother, hence Katy's Teenie's Bobby. Long ago, another name was added to the combination of family names in North-east fishing communities – the T-name. There were hundreds of T-names, and many of them survive to this day. When a community had a proliferation of family names, say, Bruces and Buchans, or Watts and Wests, and there was a limit to the number of Christian names they could use, the addition of T-names sorted things out. George 'Codlin' Cowie,' the Buckie man who featured in the Bodge and Smacker interview, was a typical example of how T-names were necessary, as were Bodge and Smacker themselves. Seventy years ago, there were well over 130 fishermen in Buckie with the name of Cowie, which meant that a large percentage of them ended up with T-names like Codlin, Cockie, Dumpy, Dosie, Fosky, Fisky, Curly, and Doddle Diddle.

In a poem, 'By Names,' in her book, *Bonnie Buchanhaven,* Gladys Milne said that some people got their T-names from their trade – Tyler Wullie and Baker Bob, for instance – and some from their home towns –

> They thocht to ca' them by that place
> Ye'd recognise the folk,
> Like Boddam Isie, English Harry,
> Buckie Meg and Jock.

'Maist names,' she said, 'came fae gweed kens far.' But the question still hung tantalisingly in the air – 'Fa had dished them oot?' The veteran Portsoy writer, Jim Slater, believes that the origin of by-name goes back to Biblical times. He quotes St Mark and the naming of the Apostles to prove it – 'And James the son of Zebedee, and John the brother of James; and he surnamed them Boanerges ...'

Sandend needed T-names more than most places, for before the war almost everyone in the village was called Smith. Back in the 1920s, no fewer than twenty-six of the fisher families in Sandend had the surname Smith, and among the owners of the eighteen boats in the port only three were *not* named Smith. Portessie was another village in which the majority of the fishermen were Smiths. Peter Anson said they came originally from Findhorn and Maviestoun. The Smiths might object to a tie-in with Maviestoun, for the folk there were disparagingly called 'fisher-gouks.'

Jim Slater told me how three John Smiths in Sandend were identified by their mothers' Christian names – Meg Low's Jock, Polly's Jock and Eppie's Jock. Two William Smiths were Kate's Wullie and Sikie's Bill, and two Bella Smiths were known as Granny's Bell and Hannah's Bell.

Some 19th century Smiths were listed in a Register of Fishing Boats covering a short period in the first half of the century. Henry Smith and his crew had two boats, as had James Smith, while George Smith and his crew had one boat. James Smith, who had six sons, built a boat for each of them. Back in 1660, one of the fishing Smiths – my namesake, Robert Smith – got his name in the record books for another reason. He was accused by the Kirk of fishing on the Sabbath.

There are still a number of Smiths in the village, although many of the houses are now owned by holiday people. 'We're getting a bit thin on the ground,' joked Jim Smith, a retired Sandend fisherman.

It was a Smith who put the village of Fordyce on the map – and helped to set other young Smiths on the road to success. George Smith, who was born in the parish, made his fortune in Bombay. In 1790, he died on his way home from India, and in his will he left money to found a school at Fordyce for teaching as many boys with the name Smith as the legacy allowed. Preference was given to those who could prove that they were related to their benefactor, down to the fourth generation of his sisters' or brothers' descendants. The result was that in 1890 four of the Smith's Bursars at Fordyce Academy were Swedes, all fourth generation descendants from George Smith's sister Jean.

Fordyce Academy built up an impressive reputation for academic success. Among its pupils were Sir James Clark, physician to Queen Victoria, and another famous medico, Sir John Forbes. In 1882 the old Academy building was converted into a house for the Rector, and to-day it is a private home. The only reminder of the Smith who became a Bombay nabob is a small plaque on the wall of the parish church.

This tiny village, tucked away at the foot of the Hill of Durn and less than two miles from Sandend, boasts a 16th century castle and an ancient, ruined church dedicated to St Tarquin. It oozes old-world charm, and I couldn't help thinking that the worst thing that could happen to it would be its discovery by hordes of tourists. Ominously, Fordyce was described in the Banff and Buchan Coastal Study as 'a significant tourist attraction.' A traditional workshop in the village has been bought by the district council, with the aim of turning it into a working interpretive facility and visitor centre, so perhaps the first crack in the dam has already appeared.

Sandend itself is beginning to show signs of suffering from tourist pressure. It is obvious that no planner's hand has touched this fisher-town. Its houses huddle, higgeldy-piggeldy, between the sea and the Braes, and that is part of its appeal, but it is marred by a caravan site that sprawls from the harbour road to the edge of the bay. Access to the beach from the village already causes parking difficulties, as the coastal Study pointed out.

Banff and Buchan District Council seem to be well aware of the problems, for they have been giving considerable thought to their future coastal policy. There is a lesson for them in Professor J. A. Steers' book, *The Coastline of Scotland,* which said that demands on the coast were always increasing. Professor Steers warned that unless the population as a whole became aware of the need to appreciate the amenities of the coast, damage would continue to increase. No part of the coast was 'safe' unless it was under the guardianship of a body capable of preventing spoliation.

Whatever lies ahead, Sandend and its neighbouring villages will continue to draw more holidaymakers. There are rich pickings for history-hungry visitors in this corner of Banffshire – the old kirk and castle at Fordyce; the spectacular ruins of Boyne Castle, the Renaissance palace near Portsoy; the early 18th century Glassaugh Windmill, restored by a local conservation group; and Glasshaugh House, once the seat of the Abercombies of Glassaugh. Before the present owners, Allan and Pat Sparring, bought Glasshaugh House, it was being used to house livestock. There were cows on the ground floor, pigs climbing the staircase to their pens on the first floor, and chickens scratching on the second floor.

Some of the places of interest are best seen from the sea. Bob Bruce, whose Orkney fastliner I had steered towards the Muckle Hoose and its drainpipe, took me on a trip along the coast. We headed across Sandend Bay to Portsoy. Lobster boats and pleasure craft are the only vessels you are likely to see in the bay to-day, but at Dunniedeich, on the east side of the bay, there are two lime kilns which were in use when sailing ships came to Sandend to pick up cargoes of lime.

Inside the Old Harbour at Portsoy, we drifted idly under Corf House, built in Portsoy's golden age in the late 17th century. A corf-house was a place for curing salmon and storing nets. This huge quayside warehouse, whose high, square windows stare unblinkingly over the Shorehead, was built by Patrick Ogilvie, later Lord Boyne, for the export of Portsoy marble to France. Chimneypieces made from Portsoy marble decorate the Palace of Versailles. To-day, marble still has a place in the old warehouse, and some of it may even end up in French hands, for Portsoy marble (serpentine) is used to make souvenirs for sale in a craft shop in Corf House.

Earlier this century, Portsoy had a declining population and a reputation as the most derelict port on the south side of the Moray Firth. In the post-war years the population rose, but it was a temporary increase, and it began to look as if the historic harbour area was plunging into terminal decay. In the 1960s, it was given the kiss of life by a prize-winning plan for the restoration of warehouses and tenements fronting the Old Harbour. Other buildings on the Shorehead were also restored, including Corf House, and to-day Portsoy can again claim to be the 'neat thriving little place' that Robert Southey found it in 1819.

We sailed out of the Old Harbour and into the new, built in the 1820s for the herring boom, swept away by a storm in 1839, and reconstructed in 1884. From there, taking a last look at the cottages that climbed up from the quayside to the Square, we turned the *Toby* away from Portsoy and headed across Sandend Bay, past the rocks at Garron Point, where Bob Bruce fished with his 'wahnie' when he was a boy.

Shags sat on the rocks drying their wings and gulls squawked and squabbled overhead as the *Toby* nosed its way up the coast. About a mile north of Sandend, where the cliffs reach heights of 90ft., a huge fist of rock sticks out into the sea. On top of it are the gaunt, impressive ruins of Findlater Castle, which can be reached by a track running from the Sandend road to the Barnyards of Findlater. There is a car park at the farm.

This 15th century fortress, clinging precariously to the rocks, was once described as a 'miniature Gibralter,' and when you see it from the sea, looking up at its great, towering cliff face, you begin to realise why. Part of the castle was actually cut out of the rocks, and the stone work of what had been the lower storeys of a central palace block can still be seen.

I wondered if this was where Sir John Gordon, a laird with a roving eye, had locked up his wife when he took a fancy to another woman – 'he castethe hys fantasie unto another,' it was reported. Some people said that the object of his 'fantasie' was Mary, Queen of Scots, and that Sir John's wife was shut away in a 'close chamber' in the castle when the Queen passed 'harde by the howse of Finlitter' with her forces in 1562, on her way north to curb the might of the Gordons.

If Findlater Castle was impregnable to attack 400 years ago, it is almost as impregnable to an 'assault' by tourists. It is not a place for coaches, and the ruins and the rock itself are dangerous. Two gaps were at one time spanned by a bridge. No carriage could reach the castle, and visitors had to approach it on foot from a forecourt laid out on the mainland.

Sunnyside Bay is in sharp contrast to gloomy Findlater. It lies west of the castle, at the Sands of Logie on the coastal path to Cullen. It is a quiet, peaceful spot, popular with picknickers. Sixty or seventy years ago. Sunday strollers often took a walk to Sunnyside to have a chat with Charlie Marioni, who was better known as Aul' Charlie, the Hermit of Cullen.

Aul' Charlie's home was a cave cut into a 50ft.-high rock almost at the sea's edge, but it was no mini-Findlater, for the last thing Charlie wanted was to keep people away. If the Queen had come riding past *his* door, he would probably have offered her a fresh-caught haddock or handed her a postcard of himself standing outside his cave. There are a number of interesting caves along this coast, among them the Preacher's Cave, which featured in George MacDonald's novel 'Malcolm,' and Farskane's Cave, where a local laird hid during the 1715 Rebellion, but the one that held Cullen's affection was Charlie's Cave.

For thirteen years, this white-bearded hermit lived in his hole in the rocks on Sunnyside Bay. He enlarged it by building an entrance made from odd scraps of wood, and later this gave way to a two-roomed shack put together from other driftwood and debris washed up on the beach. He laid out a garden and grew his own vegetables, and he caught fish from the rocks and sold them to local people.

He also had his picture taken outside his cave, posing with his fishing rod or playing his fiddle, and when a local chemist made postcards from them Charlie got himself a supply and sold them to visitors. He became a much-loved character, known for his tales and his fiddle-playing, and in the Twenties and Thirties people came from far and wide to see Aul' Charlie, the Hermit of Cullen.

Nobody knew much about his background, although they wondered at his foreign-sounding name, but it turned out that he was, in fact, a Frenchman. Then, in 1933, somebody complained that Charlie Marionic was 'breaking up ground for cultivating purposes without permission.' Inquiries were made and poor, bewildered Charlie suddenly found himself summoned to Banff Sheriff Court to answer a charge that he had failed to register as an alien when he had arrived thirteen years previously.

As it happened, he had already been recorded as an alien while living in Pembroke, and he was unaware that he had to register again when he arrived at Cullen. He pleaded guilty and was given a 20 shilling fine. He was also ordered to re-register as an alien, and Sheriff J. W. More, addressing him in French, told him that after he had paid the fine and re-registered he could carry on looking after himself as he had done before. 'Thank you,' said Charlie. 'I will go to France.'

'East, West, Home's Best,' read the inscription on one of the Sunnyside postcards, but it was no longer home to Aul' Charlie. He had made friends with scores of people during his thirteen years at Cullen, but he had been humiliated by his appearance in court. He never returned to the cave, and to-day there is little left to show that he ever lived there. Still, when you stroll along the path to Sunnyside Bay it is easy to imagine that you can hear the sound of Aul' Charlie's fiddle above the roll and rumble of the waves.

Although Charlie sold the fish he had caught on the rocks at Sunnyside, he never ate them, for he was a strict vegetarian. So he couldn't have tasted the delights of Cullen Skink, that rich, creamy soup made from smoked haddock, onion, mashed potatoes, and, it seems, whatever else happens to be handy. The broadcaster Jimmie Macgregor, writing about a trip he made along the Moray coast, described Cullen Skink as a cross between a soup and a stew. Somebody must have been chucking in too many tatties, for there is little doubt that it is a soup, not a stew. Jimmie wrote down the recipe and added, 'Anything else you fancy, if it's fishy.' Aul' Charlie would have had plenty of odds and ends to throw into his pot.

I supped my Cullen Skink inside the Seafield Arms Hotel, an old coaching inn built in 1822 by the Earl of Seafield. It cost the Earl £3000 and brought a comment from the local minister that 'the only modern building deserving of notice is the Cullen Hotel.' That couldn't be said now, for the hotel is one of a complex of striking buildings in the area known as the New Town.

Cullen's main street, Seafield Street, sweeps down towards the sea, passing the Square, the hotel, the Town Hall, and the Mercat Cross, with Cullen Bay stretching out in a wide arc in the distance. Two railway viaducts cross the main road to the north, dividing the New Town from the Seatown. The viaducts were built in 1882–84. One has eight arches, each more than 70ft. in height and with a span of 63ft., while the other has three arches. The viaducts put a distinctive stamp on Cullen, dominating the lower end of the town, and it is surprising that in the past there have been moves to have them demolished. Cullen House, built on a rock over 60ft. above the Cullen Burn, lies to the west of Seafield Street.

Time lends enchantment to the old fishertowns along the Moray coast, and Cullen is no exception. The fisher cottages huddle together as if hiding away from the storms that come raging in across the bay. The Seatown of Cullen became the Seatown of 'Portlossie' in George Macdonald's novel, *Malcolm*. He said it was 'as irregular a gathering of small cottages as could be found on the surface of the globe. They faced every way, turned their backs and gables every way – only by their roofs could you predict their position – were divided from each other by every sort of small irregular space and passage – and looked liked the National Assembly debating a constitution.'

Herring fishing was introduced at Cullen in 1815 and in 1819 Robert Southey wrote about seeing boats coming in with 300 barrels of herring caught during the night. 'Air and ocean were alive with flocks of sea fowl, dipping every minute for their share in the herring fishery. A heap of dog-fish was lying on the pier...' There were thirty-six large boats and eight skiffs in Cullen in 1839, mostly working at the herring fishing, but a decade later the herring had been abandoned and the 'haddie' had become king. At the end of last century there were five curers in the village, so it may have been then that Cullen first started making its famous Cullen Skink. By the 1920s only one curer was still operating.

West of the Seatown and across the Burn of Cullen the sands curve away to Scar Nose, which looks down on the cliff-top village of Portknockie. Cullen has a certain affinity with its neighbour, for it was a Cullen man who 'founded' it. Kathie Slater, who died in Portknockie in 1773 at the age of ninety-six, often told how her father had built the first house in the village in the same year that the Gordons had built the House of Faskane in 1677. Old Kathie said she had been brought to Portknockie from Cullen in a fisher's scull instead of a cradle.

Kathie and her father may have been Portknockie's first Slaters, but they weren't the last. Early this century there were twenty-four Slaters in the village, but in a 1960 voter's roll there were over seventy. The Woods and Mairs top the Portnockie league, the number of Woods rising from forty-seven at the start of the century to 134 in 1960, and the number of Mairs going up from eighty-nine to 220. So even after all these years the T-name game still goes on ...

CHAPTER ELEVEN
The Biggest Ice-House

The biggest ice-house in Scotland stands in the tiny village of Tugnet on the Moray Firth, only a stone's throw from the mouth of the River Spey. This semi-subterranean structure looks like a nuclear bomb shelter from the outside, for only its three rounded roofs can be seen above the ground. At the beginning of the century, wooden sheds were built over these ice house mounds. The ice house played a vital role in what was once a thriving coastal and river-based salmon fishing industry. Ice for storing the freshly-caught salmon was shovelled into it until it rose almost to its lofty ceiling.

In 1792, no fewer than twenty-four ships called at Speymouth to pick up cargoes of salmon bound for London, and over 130 men worked at the Tugnet fishing station. To-day, the salmon-catching is done by one crew, and when I was there the future looked decidedly uncertain. But whatever happens to Tugnet as a salmon-fishing station, the ice-house will continue to operate — as a museum.

Old Alex Howe, who lives in one of the Tugnet houses, was in charge of the museum. Alex was never a fisher — he spent his working life as a gardener — but his son, Ton, was formerly manager of the station. In his well-worn bonnet and crumpled waistcoat, Alex is a bit of a character. He was nearing his 90th birthday when I met him, and well set up for his century. I asked him how he had managed to reach such a ripe old age.

'I dinna smoke, I dinna drink, I dinna go wi' bad women,' he said.

Later, I saw him pulling a packet of cigarettes from his pocket and lighting one up, mentioning at the same time that he wouldn't mind a dram in the Spey Bay hotel.

So, disillusioned, I asked about his third recipe for longevity — keeping away from bad women.

'The only reason he doesn't chase women,' said Eric Goodman, one of the salmon crew, 'is that he can't catch them now.'

Eric is a bluff Yorkshireman who is really more interested in birds than fish. He has a large aviary in his back garden with five dozen wild birds ... waxwings, canaries, mannequins, and a few other exotic breeds. He takes them inside his house in the winter. Eric has been at Tugnet nearly fifteen years, and before that was at Scrabster, where he did charter work. His dog, Benny, is called after the jazz clarinettist Benny Goodman, but when Eric was in the Army everyone called *him* Benny Goodman; nobody knew him as Eric.

The Tugnet exhibition shows salmon fishing techniques, old pictures, nets, models — and a colour picture of Alex taken by a visitor. Visitors can also see an audio-visual show of the operation. In the old days, water from the River Spey was fed into shallow ponds through sluices and allowed to freeze. When the ice was thick enough fishermen broke it up with pickaxes and carried it off by horse and cart to the ice house.

The salmon crews also collected 'grue,' the thick creamy scum that formed in the eddies and backwaters of the Spey, and this was used to seal the ice. When the ice was thick enough, the cry would go up, 'Ice the morn — brogues 'n widers.' They still need waders, but not for breaking ice. The ice house was last used in 1968.

'You couldn't get the ice now, said Angus Gordon, thinking of a run of snow-less winters and long hot summers in recent years. Angus started work at the station in 1962 and became manager in 1983; before that, Tom Howe held the job for twenty years.

A board inside Angus's office is a reminder of better — and cheaper — days: 'Salmon per lb — 3s, Grilse per lb — 1s, Trout per lb — 91/2d. Terms cash.' Angus said that salmon was £1 per lb when he started. An old book records the catches of sixty years ago. The first entry reads, 'Major Grant, Glen Grant, Rothes — 1 salmon 10lb, £1 16 8d.

Current records show the decline in recent years (the figures are for 1990 and the comparisons 1989) — salmon 1753 (2000), grilse 2762 (4000), Sea trout 5334 (7000). There are a number of reasons for the decline, one of them being fish farming. Among the suggestions put forward to cope with the drop is a proposal that the spring fishing should be abandoned and the season started later, but Angus says that the fish are coming later and the season is stretching.

On the back of the door there was another notice: 'River Spey Flood Warning System.' The flood warning is still needed; a heavy spate the night before had almost brought an alert. Spates mean poor fishing, for the grilse won't go up the water. The Spey is a petulant, unruly river. Four times this century new channels have had to be cut at the river mouth to reduce the risk of flooding and to prevent the build-up of shingle. The last time this was done was in 1989. In 1991, the Scottish Office gave Grampian Regional Council a grant of £550,000 to fund coastal protection work at Kingston and Tugnet.

It was a grey, wet day when I was at Tugnet, rain scudding across the mouth of the river. Looking over the great shingle banks to Garmouth, I was thinking of the biggest spate of all, the Muckle Spate of 1829, when Garmouth and Kingston were almost swept away by the flood and the bay was littered with stranded vessels, dead animals, and drifting furniture.

The Laigh of Moray was turned into an inland sea. Findhorn, like its sister ports along the coast, was lashed by the storm. It was from Findhorn that five boats sailed over fields and hedges searching for victims of the flood. One of them, the *Nancy*, kept a record in its log-book — 'Wind blowing hard from N.N.E.; tide high, but considerably against us; sea in the bay rough, so that we shipped much water. In danger of foundering from trees and other land wreck.'

Some of the log-book entries had an almost hilarious touch. 'Set all sail, scudded, with a fair wind, over Mr Davidson's farm,' reported Donald Munro, an estate overseer and self-appointed leader of the expedition. He wore a yellow waistcoat on the trip – 'it shone amidst the chaos like the white plume of Navarre on the battlefield,' one observer said. Donald, whose colourful attire won him the permanent nickname of 'Yellow Waistcoat,' set course for a farm called Westertown of Tannochy, the

Nancy's bottom grazing the tops of the wheat, and when they got there they found the farmer's wife and her three bairns 'safely dry-docked in chairs in a bed.'

'The servants and one of the daughters were paddling about the room, *skellachin'* (shrieking) at a sad rate. The other Miss was upstairs and had gane to bed. Stowed them all away in the boat, and the bed, chest of drawers, chairs and such craft, being lightened of their cargoes, began to float through the room.' They dropped their passengers at Tannochy (now Invererne House), went south-west by Waterford and Greeshop, and at Edgefield saw 'a strange, witch-looking woman, far across in the middle o' the water.'

'We thought she waved to us,' said Donald, 'but there were currents running about her that nae boat biggit by human hands could ha' lived in, and unless she was Davy Jones' wife it is a real mystery how she could weather it.' It turned out that 'Davy Jones' wife' was, in fact, Mr Kerr, the Edgefield farmer, and he did weather it. The *Nancy* sailed from Findhorn at half-past ten in the morning, and, as the log-book recorded, 'Got to our moorings about seven o'clock p.m.'

Garmouth and Kingston, which lie about twenty miles to the east of Findhorn, have always seemed to me to be hiding away from the threat of another Muckle Spate, but both these unassuming communities have carved a niche for themselves in Moray's history. It was at Garmouth in June, 1650, that Charles II landed from Holland on his way to be crowned at Scone. The story goes that he was carried ashore on the back of a Garmouth ferryman called Milne when the boat taking him from his ship grounded in shallow water. This is a higgeldy-piggeldy little village. One early guide book said its streets and houses were 'nearly as irregular as it is possible to make them.'

If Garmouth is less than orderly, Kingston, about a mile away, can scarcely claim to be a planner's dream, yet it was laid out on a regular plan in the early 19th century, turning what had been little more than a collection of shacks into a respectable township. Down on the beach a line of cottages, sheltering behind the shingle, have their gardens backing on to the Spey's yawning estuary.

Both villages look as if they had been teased and taunted by the bullying river and then thrown aside. That, in a sense, is what happened, for the shifting Spey literally left them high and dry. Garmouth was a major port when timber was floated down the Spey for export, and Kingston was once the centre of a flourishing shipbuilding industry going back to 1786. There were seven shipyards in Kingston, but a change in shipbuilding methods, as well as the changing course of the Spey, put an end to the years of prosperity.

Standing on this deserted shore, it is hard to believe that great ships went out from Kingston to roam the oceans of the world . . . the three-masted schooner *Clansman*, which carried 620 tons of cargo; the 800-ton barque *Chieftain*, which raced — and beat — the tea clippers from Shanghai; the 300-ton brigantine *Duke of Richmond*, wrecked off Australia in 1884; and many more. The rumbling shingle banks, pushed westwards by longshore drift, are the haunt of sea birds, and an area called the Lein, bordering the beach, is now a Scottish Wildwife Trust reserve.

The coastline stretches away to Lossiemouth and the towering white finger of Covesea Lighthouse, which overlooks the huge Silver Sands Caravan Park. Moray's famous son, Ramsay MacDonald, first Labour prime minister of Britain, said that the golden sweep of sand from Lossie's Stotfield to Covesea was 'our Bay of Naples.' Covesea was originally Cousie, one of three tiny fishing hamlets which developed into the Lossiemouth of to-day. The others were Old Lossie and Stotfield. Old Lossie had one small sloop and two fishing craft, while Covesea and Stotfield each had three boats.

There was another port in this part of Moray at the end of the 14th century, in what is now landlocked Spynie. Spynie, lying on the Loch of Spynie, was 'a town and harbour inhabited by fishermen who sailed from Spynie to the sea.' In 1451 it became a burgh of barony and the following year was declared a regality 'with right of harbour and passage.' A ferry service ran from the loch to the fishing village of Cousie. By the end of the 15th century, however, the loch had become so shallow that the port became useless.

112

Spynie Palace rose majestically above the fishing port. The ruin of this mighty Bishop's Palace, which was said to be one of the finest 15th century castles in the land, has been undergoing restoration and consolidation, particularly on 'Davie's Tower,' which was built by Bishop David Stewart after the Earl of Huntly, who had been excommunicated for burning Elgin, threatened to 'pull the Bishop out of his pigeon-hole at Spynie' There is a metal gate called the Watergate in one of the walls, leading to the Loch of Spynie, but to-day it is difficult to even find the loch, which was once five miles long and over a mile wide, spreading over 2500 acres of the Laigh of Moray.

Duffus Castle, about two miles to the west, rose Leviathan-like out of the loch, but now the only water surrounding it lies in its moat. The loch was drained about 1807 so that land could be reclaimed, and local lairds called in the engineer Thomas Telford to build the Spynie Canal, which ran seven miles from near Spynie Palace to the sea at Lossiemouth. Later, a new turnpike road from Elgin to Lossiemouth was driven through the vanished loch. To-day, dead leaves and turgid water drift among the birch and rowan trees below the old road.

These old ports all have their memories, but the name Stotfield strikes unhappy chords. Stotfield has always had strong fishing traditions, but like many other seatowns it has paid a harsh price for them. The Stotfield Disaster Memorial is a sad reminder of how on Christmas Day, 1806, 'three boats containing the whole seamen of Stotfield, 21 in number, went to sea, and, a sudden storm arising, all perished.'

This kind of tragedy is not something that belongs to the past. As recently as December, 1990, three Lossiemouth brothers were members of the six-man crew of the 72 ft fishing boat *Premier* when it was swamped by mountainous seas in gale-force conditions 50 miles east of Shetland. The three other crew members were from nearly Burghead, and by a sad twist of fate the *Premier* tragedy happened almost on the 20th anniversary of the loss of the Burghead seine-net boat *Rosebud II* and her seven-man crew.

The skipper of the *Premier*, 'Ned' Edwards, and his two brothers, belonged to one of Lossiemouth's original fishing families. In 1625, one of their forbears paid eight Scottish pounds to buy a boat from Brodie of Brodie, the local laird. The family were given seven years to repay the loan.

From the shore at Lossie, the waves can be seen breaking over the Halliman Skerries. They should really be called the Holyman Skerries, for the name comes from St Gerardine, or Gernadius, a Celtic missionary, who lived in a 12 ft square cave on the sea-front. Gerardine kept a light burning in the cave on winter nights to guide local fisherman over the treacherous sandbanks, and they called him the Haly Man, hence Halliman Point and Halliman Skerries.

The coast below the cliffs of Covesea, between Lossiemouth and Hopeman, is spectacular. Nature, like some demented sculptor, has carved out a grotesque landscape in which pillars of rock, pyramids, towers and arches rise from a shoreline pitted with caves of all shapes and sizes. Isaac Forsyth, an 18th century Elgin publisher and antiquarian, wrote about the Covesea caves in his *Survey of the Province of Moray* in 1798. It was quaintly called the Muckle Isaac to distinguish it from a lesser work.

Some of the caves, said Isaac, were 'gloomily lofty,' others 'uncomfortably damp.' One cave, 'formed into a small hermitage, not exceeding 12 ft square' had a handsome Gothic door and window and 'a long but solitary view along the eastern shore.' The door and window were torn down by 'a rude shipmaster,' but Muckle Isaac gives no explanation for the shipmaster's curious act of vandalism. There was a fountain in the rock above the 'hermitage' called St Gerardine's Well, so it is almost certain that the cave mentioned in Forsyth's book was where Gerardine kept a light burning on dark winter nights.

In the fishery museum in Lossiemouth, I saw a picture postcard marked Lindsay's Cave. This was the home of a well-known tinker, George Lindsay, who lived in the cave at the end of last century. He was there for eleven years, a quiet, inoffensive man who was well-liked by the local farmers, who looked after him when he was ill. He died in 1893 at the age of seventy-four. His family had no money and George was buried by 'the sanitary authorities.'

A cave near Hopeman was known as Helg's Hole, although local people called it Hell's Hole. For years it was a home for tinkers and wandering gipsies, but other surprising characters lived in it. Early last century, William Young, the laird of Inverugie, south of Hopeman, took a visitor from the south to see Hell's Hole. When they went into the cave, one of the 'tinkers' got to his feet and greeted the laird's companion like a long-lost friend. That, in fact, was what he was. As a youth he had followed a gipsy-like existence, and in later years he periodically turned his back on respectability and went off to re-live his early life as a cave-dweller.

Some of the caves could accommodate a troop of horses. One did; it was used by a Gordonstoun laird, Sir Robert Gordon, to hide *his* horses when he wanted to prevent them from being requisitioned during the '45 Rising. The cave, which had 'a meant door' to it, is still known as Sir Robert's Stables.

The most famous of the Covesea caves is the Sculptor's Cave, which takes its name from Pictish sculpturings outlined on the walls. The cave, which was occupied from 700 BC to 500 AD, when it was apparently abandoned, faces north across the Moray Firth to the Caithness hills. Just over ten years ago, a 20-strong team headed by Grampian Region archaeologist Ian Shepherd carried out excavation work at the cave after it was discovered that it had been disturbed by treasure-hunters. The cave is difficult to find and even more difficult to reach, but the Grampian archaeologists solved the problem by building a 90 ft scaffolding tower.

The pioneering work, however, was done sixty years ago by Sylvia Benton, a Cambridge Classics graduate and teacher, who discovered the Sculptor's Cave while staying at her father's holiday home at Lossiemouth. When she was given permission to excavate it in 1929 she spent five weeks inside the gloomy cavern 'tearing lumps of clay to pieces hour after hour,' washing human bones — the floor was strewn with them — and carrying her 'finds' out of the cave in a barrow. In 1930, she did the same again.

From Ramsay MacDonald's 'Bay of Naples,' I walked across the sands and along the narrow path that leads to the Covesea caves. Off shore, the waves frothed around the Hallyman Skerries, while away to the west I could see a line of yachts slipping out of Findhorn Bay. Rafts of eider ducks bobbed up and down like corks on the water and redshanks and sandpipers scurried about the water's edge.

Then I was down on the shore and into Muckle Isaac's world of tormented rock, the sea boiling around twisted stacks and arches that he thought looked like 'broken shapeless windows in a Gothic ruin.' The Elgin antiquarian said that the whole ridge along the Covesea shore consisted of one uninterrupted mass of freestone, lying in horizontal strata, differing in thickness, colour and hardness.

At the time that Forsyth wrote his survey there were twenty masons and nearly forty labourers quarrying and cutting the stone; St Gerardine's mini-cave was destroyed during quarrying operations. A number of the stone-cutters sheltered in the caves. Forsyth thought that some of them extended well back into the hill. 'Their dark recesses have never been explored,' he added. That was two centuries ago, and most of the Covesea caves have probably now been investigated. At anyrate, I remembered Muckle Isaac's description of them as 'low, dismal, dark and damp, throughout all their windings,' and decided to leave them to the wind and waves.

CHAPTER TWELVE
Witches and Wizards

The Wizard of Gordonstoun was hard on my heels as I walked down the long, shadowy avenue to the Michael Kirk.

I resisted the temptation to look over my shoulder, remembering hideous tales of a monstrous black steed thundering through the woods with a corpse over its back. At the entrance to the church grounds, the figure of a bearded, half-naked savage carrying a heavy club over each shoulder was carved out of a stone pillar. Beyond it, ancient tombstones, flat and worn, were spread across the deserted graveyard.

The Wizard's bones lie in the mausoleum of the old kirk, which was built as a mortuary chapel by his widow, Elizabeth, when he died in 1704. Here, Sir Robert Gordon, 3rd Baronet of Gordonstoun, rests in peace, hidden away from a world that saw him as a recluse, an eccentric, a man without a shadow — a laird in league with the devil. Others saw him as a brilliant scholar born before his time, a contemporary of the scientist Robert Boyle and the Gregorys of Aberdeen.

For the past sixty years, the house where the Wizard carried out his secret work, mostly at night, has been the setting for a different kind of experiment, started in 1934 when Dr Kurt Hahn established Gordonstoun School as a school where pupils could learn independence and self-reliance as well as the three Rs. To-day, Gordonstoun is better known for its Royal 'old boys' than for any 17th century wizardy — the Duke of Edinburgh, Prince Charles and Prince Andrew were all Gordonstoun pupils.

Yet the Wizard still casts a spell over his old estate. Even in daylight an odd sort of stillness hangs over the kirk and the woods around it. Up to the middle of last century, local folk avoided the place, and even to-day few people would go there after dark. The woodland route to Michael Kirk is known as the Silent Walk and boys from the school have to walk in silence,

in single file, when they attend church services there. Prince
Charles was struck by what he called the 'magnetism' of the
kirk. It had, he said, 'a peculiar kind of eerie mystery which
no Gordonstoun boy will ever forget.'

The biggest mystery of all is whether or not Sir Robert did, in
fact, tamper with the supernatural. Firelight flickered from the
window of his ground-floor laboratory in Gordonstoun House
when decent folk were in their beds, and they wondered what
went on in that mysterious workshop. His secret experiments
won him the nickname of 'The Wizard.' He was a recluse; his
neighbours seldom saw him. His servants held him in awe,
partly because of his nocturnal activities, and partly because
of his reputation as their laird.

He was a product of the 17th century, with absolute power
over his people, and at times he used it with a good deal of
brutality. He held his own court, and the worst miscreants were
thrown into a water dungeon in Gordonstoun House and left
to die among the rats. On one occasion he had a woman tied
to the back of the local ferryboat and then stood on the shore
and watched her drown.

In 1665, he was sent to Italy to study at the University of
Padua, and it was during his time there that he is supposed to
have summoned the Devil and bartered his soul for the secrets
of the universe. Gordon tried to avoid keeping his part of the
bargain — when Auld Nick came to claim his soul, he pointed
to his shadow on the wall and said, 'Take that fellow instead.'
The Devil, amused, said that he could have 25 years without
his shadow — and *then* he would come for his soul.

Back in his home in Moray, Gordon stayed indoors when
the sun shone; that way, nobody noticed that he was a man
without a shadow. A poem written by William Hay in 1839
described how the Devil finally claimed his prize. It pictured
the De'il and Sir Robert drinking together — 'a man has sma'
chance that would drink wi' the Deil' — and went on to tell
how Satan turned into a 'fierce-looking charger' and carried
the Laird off on his back. The post commented —

Losh! sic a queer loon
Was this Morayshire loon!

There is little doubt that Sir Robert *was* a queer loon, but his credulous servants turned his eccentricity into something more sinister. The so-called Wizard was obsessed with scientific study and research, and in that 'devil's furnace' in his laboratory he produced some fine examples of the blacksmith's art.

Some say that his greatest piece of 'magic' was the Round Square, built about 1690 as a stable-block. It was said to be designed in the form of a magic circle so that the Devil would never be able to get Sir Robert into a corner. Henry Brereton, in his book, 'Gordonstoun,' described it as 'a scientific sanctuary for his soul.' To-day, it houses classrooms and a library.

The Wizard's son was known as Ill Sir Robert, not because he had bad health, but because he was ill-tempered. He fell out with his neighbours, treated his tenants cruelly, and behaved badly to his wife, Agnes. Agnes, however, gave him as good as he got. He shut her up in the dungeon to teach her a lesson, but when that didn't work he fell back on an old superstition which said that if you built a doocot your wife died. Ill Sir Robert, taking no chances, built four of them, including a magnificent specimen which can be seen near the Round Square. Obviously that didn't work either, for Agnes outlived him.

Not everybody regards Michael Kirk as an eerie place. Edward Lightowler, who wrote a book on the kirk, said it was 'a haven of peace,' and that deep in the heart of every 'old boy' lay a mysterious love for it. Sadly, the peace is broken by the ear-shattering roar of aircraft from the airfield at Lossiemouth, which come low over Gordonstoun House and Michael Kirk. No doubt they would have greatly intrigued the mechanically-minded Sir Robert, but when I was inside the kirk I found it difficult to imagine how anyone could even hear a service there. It was a sound I was to hear again as I went along the coast, passing Kinloss, where a road sign tells you, not to watch out for cars, but to keep an eye open for aircraft lumbering into the air over Findhorn Bay.

Findhorn, straggling along the edge of the bay, is another village whose size and appearance give no hint of its importance in former years, yet it was once the main seaport in Moray. It had a number of boats trading with Aberdeen and London, as well as the Continent, bringing in wines, silks and tapestries for the Moray lairds and exporting beef, salmon, grain and malt. Now the big boats have gone and Findhorn has become famous as a yachting centre. The man behind the founding of the Royal Findhorn Yacht Club was a local worthy called Jim Chadwick, who in 1930 allowed his house to be used by yachtsmen as a clubhouse.

'Chaddy,' who had side-whiskers, a large walrus moustache, and a curly pipe with a tin top on it, designed what became known as the Findhorn boats. There were thirteen of them, but the number 13 was never used. The Findhorn boat-building tradition is carried on to-day in the shed where the prototype of 'Chaddy's' 18 ft boat was built. Here, Norman Whyte builds salmon cobbles, loch dinghies and pleasure-craft for customers as far afield as Cornwall.

There is a breath of the past in a picture of old sailing ships on the wall of his workshop — ninety-niners, said Norman. They were called that because if you had a vessel of over 100 tons there were special regulations to follow, including the provision of an extra certificated officer. So everyone built their vessels up to 99 tons.

There have actually been three Findhorns. The shifting mouth of the river, like the ever-changing Spey, led to the village twice being rebuilt on a new site. The people here are used to Nature's tantrums. They have a permanent reminder in front of them of what, apart from the Muckle Spate, was the biggest disaster ever to hit Moray. Looking across the bay, I thought of Andrew Young's poem on the Culbin Sands —

> Here lay a fair fat land;
> But now its townships, kirks, graveyards,
> Beneath bald hills of sand
> Lie buried deep as Babylonian shards.

It was through this fair fat land, along the fringe of the Culbin Forest, that I made my way to Maviston, three miles east of Nairn. Three or four centuries ago, the folk of Maviston were branded as 'fisher gouks' because they were said to be superstitious, ignorant and lazy. There are certainly no 'gouks' there now, because Maviston has disappeared from the map. This was where thousands of acres of good farming land in the meal girnel of Moray were buried under mountains of sand during the terrible Culbin disaster.

In the autumn of 1694, after sandhills at Maviston had been weakened by people pulling up marram grass to thatch their cottages, they were swept eastwards by a succession of fierce gales. The sand, 100 ft deep in places, buried everything in its path, choking the mouth of the River Findhorn. James Lorimer, in his novel, *The Fortune of the Sands*, described how a Maviston tenant burst in on Alexander Kinnaird, the Culbin laird. 'For God's sake, Laird,' he cried, 'gaither the men at the mains an' come tae oor help or oor ferm toon'ill be smoored i' the sand. It's a broken loose from the hills o' Mavieston and is coming' doon upo' us like a deluge.'

The recovery from that 'deluge' of sand is something of a miracle. Work on the reclamation of Culbin began in 1870 and in 1921 the Forestry Commission began systematic replanting. Now the whole area is massively afforested, woodlands stretching some eight miles along the coast and two miles inland. There is no sign of the 'fisher gouks' village; the only place you will see the name Maviston now is at the entrance to Maviston Farms. Sandy Cameron, who bought the farms when he retired from Inverness in 1979, said he had never found the remains of the village. He doubted if anything was left.

He was told that it had been on the north side of Loch Loy, which is almost at the bottom of his garden. He took me into his lounge, where we stood watching a pair of swans moving gracefully over the loch's placid waters. Beyond the loch was Culbin Forest. If we could have turned the clock back three centuries we would have been looking on to the sea and the Maviston sandhills, and perhaps even on to the 'lost' village itself. From the window you can see ships passing along the firth; at times, it looks as if they were actually riding on top of the trees.

Two miles east of Maviston is Brodie Castle, where, although you are unlikely to find any gouks or wizards, you may find a skeleton in the cupboard. It was actually hanging from a wall when I was there, and a note beside it said it was a 'medical specimen' thought to have belonged to the 21st Brodie of Brodie. This local laird had something in common with the Wizard of Gordonstoun, for he was also interested in science. He was a Fellow of the Royal Society and a gentleman amateur scientist. Apparently, he had a species of flower named after him.

The last time I was at Brodie Castle there were two Brodies at the entrance. The *living* Brodie was sitting beside a full-size portrait of himself by David Anderson. This time the flesh-and-blood Brodie was on his own, selling tickets to incoming customers, but he pointed out that his 'double' was just around the corner. How do you address a Brodie of Brodie? Mr Brodie? Somehow or other, it didn't seem right, and I wondered if I should call him 'Laird.' In fact, his correct title is *The* Brodie, and he should be addressed simply as Brodie. American visitors, accustomed to first-name familiarity, are taken aback when they are told to call him 'Brodie.'

Brodie Castle is run by the National Trust, and Brodie of Brodie often walks around the castle with his visitors, telling them about its history. They say he is a very affable chap. He still lives in the castle and likes to meet people. There have been Brodies at Brodie since 1160, and the oldest part of the present castle dates from about 1430. Robbie Burns spent a night there in 1787.

From Brodie I went off to see the fisher folk of Nairn. Peter Anson once said that Nairn townspeople looked down 'with a superior condescension and tolerance' on the fishers,' and I wondered if that was still true. Margaret Bochel, who helps to run the Nairn Fishertown Museum, told me that when she was a child people spoke about the *uptoonies* and the *doontoonies* — the *doontoonies* were the fishers, and the *uptoonies did* look down on them. In the old fishertown, I thought that the *doontonies* were trying to put themselves on a higher social plane by calling one of their streets Society Street.

There was, in fact, a whole series of Society Streets, each branching off the main one, with the house numbers marked on the street sign.

This system of having a main street and similarly named sub-streets seemed to me to be a postie's nightmare, but it appears to work. The same thing happens in Park Street, as I found when I wandered around the fishertown searching for Margaret Bochel, who lives at No. 52 Park Street. There were Park Streets to the left, Park Streets to the right — Park Streets everywhere. The fact that Bochel is about as common a name as Smith didn't help — 'Bochel, Bunker and Duggie' were at one time the most common names in Nairn, according to Peter Anson. They were T-names, brought into use because of the confusing number of Mains in Nairn.

'Everybody's ca'ad Bochel here,' said one helpful lady. Everybody is also called Margaret. I began by looking for Margaret Bochel, who some time ago wrote about the history of the Fishertown of Nairn, but she was off on holiday to America. The best thing to do, I was told, was to look up Margaret Bochel's cousin. What was her name, I asked. 'Margaret Bochel,' came the reply.

It was *this* Margaret Bochel, the one at No. 52 Park Street, who told me that the word 'Society' had nothing to do with snobbery. The street, or streets, were called after the Nairn Fishermen's Society, which was formed in 1767 to look after the welfare of those marked down in the first minute book as 'the Semen (sic) of Nairn.' The members paid in 'quarterpennys' four times a year to society funds.

The fortunes of the fishers have fluctuated. In 1855 there were 150 boats and 410 fishermen, but by 1881 the figure had dropped to ninety-one boats and 245 boys and men. By 1927 there were forty-one boats, of which twenty-four were steam drifters. To-day, there is only one Nairn fishing boat, the *Strathnairn*, skippered by David Main, which is registered at Inverness and fishes out of other ports.

There is a striking photograph in the Fishertown Museum showing Nairn harbour in 1900, with Zulu fishing boats rubbing shoulders with a coastal schooner. Now, the harbour is full of pleasure craft and there is little, if anything, to stir memories of the old days. Here, the building of a multi-million pound residential retail and leisure complex at the harbour has effectively demolished the past, which is a pity. The fishermen's 'Parliament,' where dreamy-eyed old salts sat and reminisced about how things were in the old days, has been swept away by the new development.

The atmosphere of the old town lingers on in the Fishertown itself, although few fisher families still live there. Many of the houses have been modernised, but some retain links with the fishing years. On the gable of Margaret Bochel's house, for instance, there is a high wooden shed where nets were pushed through a window to await repair either there or in a room of the house.

The Seamen's Victoria Hall, built in 1887, is a solid monument to the past. Nowadays, they play indoor bowls in it, but at one time it was where the Fishertown weddings were held. The first to take place was in December, 1887, and, being the first, there was no charge.

Margaret still has receipts from the wedding of her parents — 'Mr Hugh Bochel and Miss Baillie' — in 1921, when her father paid £12 12s for a frock coat, £2 for a pair of boots — and £2 5s for a tile hat. The tile hat is still there, with the initials HMB and £2 5s seen faintly on the inside rim. It is a unique hat, because it was used at Hugh Bochel's wedding *and* his funeral. The funeral took place on January 15, 1943, when Nairn was hit by a bad storm. Margaret's Uncle John had no hat to protect him from the weather, so Hugh's old tile hat was dug out and a piece of felt cut out of it so that it could fit Uncle John's head. After that, the old hat followed its former owner to the burial service.

Weddings were grand affairs in the lum hat era. At the first wedding in 1887, the local grocer sent a large box of conversation lozenges as a gift to the bride, starting a custom that continued for years at weddings in the Seamen's Hall. The men picked out the most romantic lozenges to give to their partners, and there was a scramble to get those with the motto 'I Love you.' The last loving lozenge was sucked dry in October, 1938, when the Seamen's Hall opened its doors for the last time as a venue for Fishertown weddings. Despite the changes that have taken place in recent years, Nairn's fisherfolk cherish their past, and the Fishertown's story is on permanent record in the museum at the Laing Hall, which was visited by over 2000 people in 1990.

There is a different kind of change west of Nairn. On both sides of the town great sand-bars stretch along the seaboard, the one to the west bordering the Carse of Delnies and running in a long peninsula to Whiteness Head. It acts as a breakwater to McDermott's platform production yard at Ardesier, and when I passed the yard I could see the skeleton of a huge oil rig silhouetted against the sky. It was from this site that the Piper Field production platform Oxy was launched, and I thought of Peter Buchan — Andrew's Oxy's Peter — who told me that because of his T-name he was the *real* owner of Occidental.

Farther west, where the village of Ardersier swings in a straggling line around the long arc of the bay, Fort George pushes out into the Firth like a spearhead, reaching towards Chanonry Point, where a lighthouse blinks its message a mile away on the Black Isle. This was where my journey ended. It had started with witches and warlocks shrieking across the Slunks of St Cyrus, and it ended with a witch. Between Ardersier and Nairn there is a farm called Drumdivan, where, in the 17th century, the Thane of Cawdor fell from his horse and died. They blamed it on witchcraft, and a poor old crone was arrested because she 'looked not like an inhabitant of this earth.' They burned her at the stake.

Standing on the shore at Fort George, looking over the firth to the misty hills of Cromarty, I was thinking less about witches and wizards than about the long, tortuous trail I had taken from the Montrose Basin. I had travelled through a fascinating part of the North-east, seeing braw towns and busy people; I had dropped in on quaint old villages that for generations had clung precariously to the land, and I had learned about a country rich in history and tradition and enriched in a different way by the friendly folk who live there — *uptoonies* and *doontoonies*. Change and so-called progress have put a deadening hand on some of these coastal communities, but I met plenty of people who will fight hard to retain their heritage. I wish them well.

FURTHER READING

Alexander, William, *Johnny Gibb of Gushetneuk*. Douglas, 1912.

Allan, John R., *The North-east Lowlands of Scotland*, Hale, 1952.

Fraser, Amy Stewart, The Hills of Home. Routledge & Kegan Paul, 1981.

Fraser, Duncan, *Portrait of a Parish*. Standard Press, 1970.

Graham, Cuthbert, *Portrait of Aberdeen and Deeside*. Hale, 1972.

Gibbon, Lewis Grassic, *A Scots Quair*. Hutchinson, 1946.

Lightowler, Edward, *The Michael Kirk, Gordonstoun*. Paul Harris, 1980.

Macgregor, Jimmie, *The Moray Coast, Speyside and the Cairngorms*. BBC Books, 1987.

McKean, Charles, *Banff and Buchan*. Mainstream, 1990.

McKean, Charles, *The District of Moray*. Scottish Academic Press, 1987.

Michie, Mary, *A Tourist Guide to Aberdour Shore*. P. Scroggie, 1986.

Smith, J.S. and Stevenson, D. (editors), *Fermfolk & Fisherfolk*. Aberdeen University Press, 1989.

Thompson, *Francis, Portrait of the Spey*. Hale, 1979.

Tranter, Nigel, *The Queen's Scotland*. Hodder & Stoughton, 1972.

Summers, David W., *Fishing off the Knuckle*. Centre for Scottish Studies, 1988.

Index